PRAISE FOR DR. DEANGELA BURNS-WALLACE AND *MADE FOR THIS*

"This work reminds us that few reach success without the support of immediate and extended family. From the first uncertain steps of childhood to the winding roads of adulthood, this memoir is a tapestry woven from moments of laughter, heartbreak, and discovery. With candor and wit, the author invites you into her world—where ordinary days turn extraordinary and every setback carries the seed of renewal. Through family tales, personal triumphs, and unexpected detours, these pages offer a deep human exploration of resilience and hope.

"Deepak Chopra's concept of 'synchrodestiny' is evident in every chapter.

"Tender, unflinching, and moving, this memoir reminds us that the path to understanding oneself is rarely straight and never dull. Step inside and discover a life honestly lived and one which verifies we must lift as we climb."

—Harriet L. Elam-Thomas,

US Ambassador (Ret.)

"Reading *Made for This* feels like sitting down with a trusted friend who's willing to share the real story—the victories, the doubts, and the moments in between. DeAngela Burns-Wallace writes with honesty, humor, and grace, offering lessons that resonate far beyond the page. This book isn't just for leaders—it's for anyone ready to embrace their full, authentic self."

—Rich Bracken,

Founder, Unstoppable Solutions

"It's a rare day when someone can share so honestly the depths and peaks of struggles while also recognizing how to harness the power of your underlying ecosystem of contributors for meaningful personal and professional success. Using direct and simple storytelling, DeAngela provides a masterclass in learning lessons from the past to chart your best journey forward. Or more simply put: Because I believe no one wins alone, this is one of the most inspiring books I've ever read."

—Julie Lorenz,

Former leader of the Kansas Department of Transportation

Made for This

DR. ANGELA
BURNS-WALLACE
EdD

Made for This

LESSONS IN LEADERSHIP, LEGACY, AND LIVING UNAPOLOGETICALLY

Advantage | Books

Published by Advantage Books, Charleston, South Carolina.
An imprint of Advantage Media.

Printed in the United States of America.

10 9 8 7 6 5 4 3 2 1

ISBN: 979-8-89188-442-7 (Hardcover)
ISBN: 979-8-89188-299-7 (Paperback)
ISBN: 979-8-89188-300-0 (eBook)

Library of Congress Control Number: 2025925448

Cover design by Matthew Morse.
Layout design by Ruthie Wood.

This publication is designed to provide accurate and authoritative information in regard to the subject matter covered. It is sold with the understanding that the publisher is not engaged in rendering legal, accounting, or other professional services. If legal advice or other expert assistance is required, the services of a competent professional person should be sought.

02-24-2026 11:0

To my son, Xavier.

You are my joy, motivation, and inspiration, always. Continue to shine brightly and walk your own path. In your eyes, I see the future, and it is bright.

With love and pride.

"Perhaps you were born for such a time as this." —Esther 4:14

"When I stand before God at the end of my life, I would hope that I would not have a single bit of talent left but could say I've used everything you gave me." —Erma Bombeck

Esther and Erma set the stage …

CONTENTS

FOREWORD

ade for This is a memoir by DeAngela Burns-Wallace that captures the life story of a determined, success-bound, female African American who overcame many unpredictable obstacles along the way that might have stymied anyone else. Not DeAngela. She is a powerhouse, and her story is an instructive, alluring must-read for the young who are finding their way in today's complicated and rapidly changing professional world and for older generations who will glean insight into the depth of influence they can and should exert on succeeding generations. Throughout this riveting manuscript, DeAngela's character shines through as an impressive leader who is devoted to mentoring, bringing about systemic improvements, and generally making the world a better place.

Born in the center of America's heartland, DeAngela was brought up by unforgettable relatives, including the indomitable Aunt Peaches; a hard-charging, impeccably honest father; and an industrious, creative mother, all of whom instilled in her a sense of self-confidence that would serve her well as she embarked on her professional life, beginning with her assignments in the Foreign Service. It was during her first overseas assignment to China that she learned fundamental lessons of leadership that would serve her well throughout her career. I met DeAngela while serving as director of the US State Department's Foreign Service Institute (FSI), which trains diplomats for overseas duty. Her enthusiasm and commitment to FSI's training and her obvious intelligence made her a standout who attracted my attention. Consequently, it was my pleasure to become her mentor and to follow her career in the Foreign Service, academia, state government, the private sector, and now philanthropy.

Readers will be mesmerized by her very successful and exciting time in the Foreign Service, where she learned to speak Chinese, experienced post-apartheid South Africa, and was advised by luminaries such as Ambassador Susan Rice. Then she stepped out on faith into the world of academia. There, she excelled at Stanford University, the University of Missouri, and the University of Kansas. Readers will be inspired by her passion for improving student success and expanding educational access to students of color. DeAngela's experiences shed light on the fact that without diverse voices at the leadership table, organizations are not equipped to deal with the issues of race, equity, and inclusion. DeAngela always claimed a seat at the table, bringing creative, workable solutions to intractable problems.

I was proud to watch as DeAngela assumed her duties as secretary of administration for the state of Kansas, where she adeptly changed the perception of the Department of Administration from a convenient entity for other government departments to blame for their own shortcomings to one that was perceived as a solution finder, not a hindrance. DeAngela's handling of the divisiveness and other work-related problems that arose during COVID-19 demonstrated true leadership worthy of emulation.

Throughout the story of her life, DeAngela placed emphasis on family and friends—her son, Xavier, is the pride of her life. Her parents are an integral part of her support system, and the friends, mentors, and professional colleagues who have helped her along the way all come together to provide her with the strength to succeed and to become an unforgettable force of nature whose positive influence on those she interacts with makes an indelible impression. This book leaves the reader inspired, with many useful ideas on how to approach life successfully while helping others do the same.

—Ambassador Ruth A. Davis

About Ambassador Davis

Ruth A. Davis was a distinguished American diplomat who broke barriers throughout her forty-year career. She was the first woman to serve as senior watch officer in the Operations Center (1982–1984), the first African American to lead the Foreign Service Institute (1997–2001), and the first African American woman to become director general of the Foreign Service (2001–2003). Ambassador Davis also achieved the rank of career ambassador, being the only African American woman to do so, and held this title longer than any other officer. In 2016, she was honored with the American Foreign Service Association's Lifetime Contributions to American Diplomacy award.

Upon retirement, Ambassador Davis was the highest-ranking Foreign Service officer. Even in retirement, she remained active, holding leadership roles in various organizations that advocated for women's economic empowerment and promoted the recruitment and retention of individuals of color in the Foreign Service. She passed away on May 3, 2025, eight months after reading this manuscript and writing this foreword. I am most thankful for her contribution.

INTRODUCTION

THE CHAMPION

"The Champion"

I was made for this
I was born to win
I am the champion

—Carrie Underwood, featuring Ludacris

or the first time in my life, I took a pause.

As a good friend of mine has termed it, an intentional pause. A time to step away from work and various responsibilities and to focus on *the future* me and mine. And what did I do during this pause? I decided to write a book. Doesn't sound like much of a pause, does it?

Made for This has been a true labor of love. A labor of love that has invoked deep joy and residual pain (and maybe just a bit of therapy). My journey is one of love, loss, triumph, and remembrance. Over the years, I have chosen to openly share pieces of my journey in conversations and keynotes. Then there are other pieces that I have chosen to only share with family and friends closest to me because opening yourself up to share beyond what people see in a quick post on social media is not an easy task.

I began the writing of this book in much the same way. When I first sat down with my editor, I told her, "This book is going to be a series of lessons in leadership." I had outlined chapters and ten clear leadership tenets that would drive the narrative. The whole book was centered around those tenets, from the chapter titles to how we organized the stories to the research. It was going to be a leadership-inspired memoir driven by my leadership lessons, first and foremost, and my personal stories as backdrops to the lessons. But as the stories unfolded, I realized that I was using the leadership tenets as a mask to hold back and to only share what fit nicely with my public image.

But as a leader, I have come to understand that it is imperative that we share not only the triumphs but also the vulnerabilities, doubts, challenges, and failures that bring us to those triumphs, for they are necessary pieces of everyone's journey.

As those personal stories came to life, so too did the individuals involved, along with the realization that some parts of my journey were also other people's stories and that not all the stories were mine to tell. I worked hard to ensure that it was my perspective, my understanding, and my lived experiences that were written on the pages that follow. I did my best to keep everyone as whole as possible, allowing them to hold their own stories and tell their truths.

The process of writing this book invoked its own doubts, challenges, and, yes, triumphs (my book has made it into your hands!). When I took a step back early in the process, I doubted if anyone would even want to read my story. My story doesn't feel remarkable or special to me; I'm not a famous household name or celebrity. My godsister helped me cast those doubts aside when she said, "You are an inspiration. It is an honor to know you and be a part of your journey. You have so much to share; never doubt that."

Further along in the writing process, when my editor and early readers uncovered my masks, I was challenged to dig deeper and reveal myself more fully. It was not easy, but I pushed myself to meet those challenges.

So, who am I? I am a leader. I am a woman. I am a Black woman. I am a mother. I am a sister. I am a daughter. I am an aunt. I am a cousin. I am a friend. I am a partner. I am a mentor. I am a mentee. I am an educator. I am a policymaker. I am a philanthropist. I am an author. I am just me. We are each unique, multifaceted, and powerful beings that move through this life trying to learn, connect, love, and dream. I am honored and humbled to share my unique journey with you. One that I hope inspires you, makes you think, and validates not only who you are but who you want to be.

My story is grounded in leadership, legacy, and living unapologetically. If you are a newly emerging leader or one looking for renewal and inspiration, I hope you enjoy the ride!

About the Music ...

I walk through life with a soundtrack always playing in my head. Music touches people in the purest way. The intro, the first lyrics, or the string of a particular instrument takes you back to childhood memories, high school dances, college friends, family events, and moments of a lifetime. Each chapter is titled with a song, and each chapter opens with a few lines from that song. I hope you hear my soundtrack as you walk with me through my story, and I hope you create your own soundtrack to inspire you along the way. Enjoy!

CHAPTER 1
FAMILY FIRST

"Family First"

Nothing's better than family,
For the ones who love you so

—Whitney Houston, Cissy Houston, Dionne Warwick, and family

One of my earliest memories is helping pick tomatoes from my granny's garden out back as a small child and setting them on the windowsill to watch them turn from green to red. Red meant we could shake a little salt on them and eat them like apples. That was the best. Everyone was welcome to Granny's tomatoes, along with all the other food she grew or made. When you walked into her dining room, the white roaster oven was always filled with chicken and dumplings or turkey and dressing, sitting there warm and ready, and under her glass cake holder was always a homemade German chocolate cake or sweet potato pie. There was always something cooking and something to eat for everyone at Granny's.

Granny's kind smile and deep, full laugh were as welcoming as the delicious aromas that wafted through the kitchen. Her skin was the color and smoothness of caramel, and when she'd tell us to go "warsh your hands in the zinc," her Dumas, Arkansas, drawl was unmistakable. Granny was my dad's mom. Her name was Fannie Mae Ford, but everyone called her Aunt Peaches. She was the person everyone in the family, the church, and the neighborhood went to if they were in need.

When family members came in from out of town, it was time to take care of them. That meant Granny cooked nonstop. Fish of all types—whiting, buffalo, and catfish—would always be in the sink or the fryer beside large pots of spaghetti. On every available surface in the house or on the porch, adults played backgammon, spades, bid whist, or dominoes. We kids took turns cranking the homemade ice cream maker, and when it wasn't our turn, we were back playing freeze tag in the yard. For some families, this may only happen on a holiday or a special occasion. For my family, this is how Granny taught us to welcome those we loved—our family and friends—every day.

If Granny couldn't offer help herself, she called on others to help. When my dad transferred home to a local college, trying to finish his degree, he was working a full-time job, but he could not afford his schoolbooks. With me on the way, Granny told Dad's older brother, "Go pay for that boy's books." And he did. Several years later, my aunt's car broke down, and she needed help making car payments on a new vehicle. Granny called Dad and said, "Jerome, help your sister with her payments." And he did, even while working overtime to provide for his own family.

My dad said he learned to treat people with dignity, respect, and care because of Granny. It was just her way; it became his way and my way.

My dad, Jerome, or JB as many called him on the job, worked long hours as a telephone repairman. He was the one who came into your home and fixed the phone jack and climbed the poles outside of your house to make sure you could communicate with your family and friends. The telephone was a utility back then in a way that is different now. Before cell phones, when phone lines went down, it meant people could only connect in person. There were no alternatives to calling on the phone—no email or social media. No means to call in case of an emergency meant the telephone was a critical utility that required my dad to sometimes work nights, weekends, and holidays. My granny lived in the city, right around the corner from where my dad worked, and I remember my dad would work the morning of a holiday and then come over to my granny's house, and all the family would be there. He'd go upstairs and take a shower and change into the clean clothes my mom brought him. Then he'd come down and eat. Being in the service industry meant you had to get your job done; you had to take care of the people. For my dad, that meant the people he worked with too.

Back then, the crew my dad worked with was predominately white and male, yet they served a predominately Black inner-city neighborhood. It was the neighborhood my father grew up in and my granny still lived in. I remember in my early teens, the late eighties, being introduced to a new colleague of my dad's, Kim. She had transferred to the crew with some trepidation—about the crew demographics and new, unfamiliar neighborhoods to navigate. She immediately gravitated to my dad, asking him for assistance and information and going out to lunch with him to learn more. My dad later learned that, before transferring, Kim had asked around about whom she should connect with to ease her transition. She had been told time and time again, "Start with Burns. He's a good guy." When my dad shares this story, he quickly adds, "I was raised to be a helpful person. If I can help you, I will."

My mom, Mary, is as giving as my dad. She started her higher education at what was then called Central Missouri College, but in the early 1970s, a young Black woman studying art was not encouraged. She returned home after her freshman year and enrolled in a premier interior design school in Kansas City. She completed the program, which guaranteed a job in the interior design field, but my mom, the only Black student, was also the only graduate who was never placed and who never received her certification. Soon enough, she had a family to help support and bills to pay, and she found work as an accounting clerk. My mom excelled at her job, and she worked for some major corporations during her career.

My mom never gave up on her real dreams or lost her creativity or passion for art. When she was in her forties, she started her own event planning business that delivered spectacular events for more than six hundred guests at venues as large as the Chiefs' Arrowhead Stadium in Kansas City, Missouri. An amazing artist who freely shares her gifts, my mom has used her talents to create and sell crafts throughout the years. But mostly, she uses them to celebrate and acknowledge important milestones in the lives of those she loves. For years, she has created and sent handcrafted cards to family and friends. During the pandemic, she created more than two hundred cards and just as many masks for me to send out to staff and colleagues to help encourage them during those challenging times.

I grew up watching my parents work hard every day, and they instilled that work ethic in me and my brother, Jason. They also instilled an acknowledgment and understanding that everyone is important and that everyone has value and should be treated as such. Our extended families on both sides lived those same values. If a family member, friend, or neighbor needed help, we helped. It's just what we did.

I remember helping my mom pack up food to bring to family or friends. My mom and dad purchased a cow each year, and each year they shared half of that cow with my mom's sister's family, never worrying about the cost and only helping to meet family members' needs. When I was around twelve, one of my cousins was in a life-threatening situation halfway across the country, and her mother did not have the means to get to her quickly. My parents took money out of their savings to fly my aunt there to pick up her child and fly them both back home. I remember thinking, "My daddy can help save everyone." I can hear my dad say, as he so often does, "That's just how I was raised."

My parents didn't have to tell me how to treat people; they lived it for me to see every day, and my parents and my granny made sure my brother and I were surrounded by people who shared those same values—values that were born of and nourished by our faith.

So much of how our family moves through the world is rooted in our faith. Being a proud, Black, God-fearing woman, Granny was passionate in her commitment to treating everyone with kindness. She was a founding member of Paradise Missionary Baptist Church in Kansas City, Missouri. My dad came up in that church, and my mom, once they got married, joined that church. They would bring my brother and me up in that church. I would get married in that church. Paradise was my granny's everything, and the community she built within her church would impact my life in so many ways, including providing me with my first taste of what it felt like to lead.

CHAPTER 2
GRATEFUL

"Grateful"

Grateful, grateful, grateful, grateful
Grateful, grateful, grateful, grateful
Grateful, grateful, grateful, gratefulness is flowing from my heart

—Hezekiah Walker and the Love Fellowship Choir

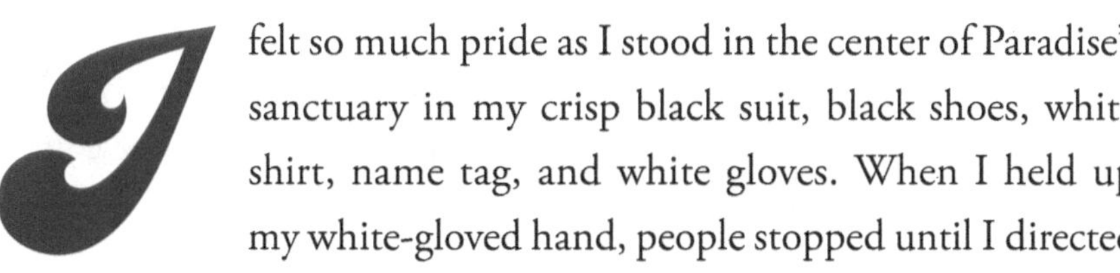

I felt so much pride as I stood in the center of Paradise's sanctuary in my crisp black suit, black shoes, white shirt, name tag, and white gloves. When I held up my white-gloved hand, people stopped until I directed them where to go. When the pastor was ready to receive the offering or to pray over the congregation, it was the ushers whom he signaled to pass the offering baskets or shut down the aisle. I was one of those ushers. Ushers controlled the flow of the sanctuary, and the adults had to listen to them, no matter how little or young they were. Many of my friends sang in the choir. I would say, "Y'all can go sing up in the choir if y'all want to." I didn't care that I couldn't sing because being an usher—being in charge—was so much better.

Pulling on my pristine white gloves just before taking my post on Youth Sundays filled me with so much confidence and joy. Those gloves were the final touch to my usher uniform. A uniform of authority. A uniform that commanded respect.

It was heavy stuff for a kid, and it was not a game. It was a serious responsibility that came with high expectations. As a youth usher, I watched the adult ushers closely. I wanted to look as crisp and clean as they did, to stand as straight as they did, and to perform my duties in exactly the way they did. I made sure my offering tray was ready with neatly stacked envelopes and that the folds in my programs were just so. Ushers didn't just hand out the programs; we were also in charge of putting the programs together. I remember collecting the freshly printed pages from the secretary's office in the back of the church and then laying the pages one on top of the other before putting one staple exactly in the middle to hold them all together. We would then take great pains to fold along that staple and crease the programs just the right way. The lead usher's folds were on point, and I was determined that mine would be too.

On Youth Sundays, which were the fourth Sunday of every month, all aspects of the church services were run by us kids. We read scriptures, did the announcements, led prayers, and, of course, ushered and sang in the choir. It was a natural expectation at Paradise that, as a member of the community, no matter your age, you had to be a responsible and engaged member. You had to show up in a certain way, and we were encouraged and empowered to do so at every turn.

My mom was very active in coordinating the youth program, and so, my brother and I would spend our summers at Paradise with my mom. Jason is five years younger than me. That meant I was an only child for the first five years of my life. I'll be honest; gaining a sibling was an adjustment for me. While I don't have any memory of this, my mom says I dropped Jason on his head a lot when he was little. Because of our age difference, our time in school, our friends, and our interests never really overlapped. But church was different because it was about family and community, and regardless of age, we were all immersed together in one way or another. In those spaces together, Jason felt it was his job to report to my mother any small infraction I may have made—even something as small as talking to a boy for "too long." At home, he was the typical little brother who would stand in the hallway, with his toes perfectly lined up at the edge of my door, goading me to yell, "Get out of my room!" (which I always did) so he could then point at his feet and say, "I'm not in your room."

During those growing-up years, I thought of Jason in the same way that most of my friends thought of their younger siblings: They were pests to be barely tolerated. When we grew into adulthood, that five-year gap became insignificant, and I came to appreciate the caring, strong, and intelligent human being my brother had always been. But until then, I made little time for him. And of course, I always tried to sneak away from him during those fun, hot summers.

The summer youth program that my mom and other youth leaders put together was much broader than a typical summer vacation Bible school. We had all kinds of activities at the church, including mini sports tournaments, game nights, meal preparations, and so much more.

We also had the opportunity, as members of the youth ministry at Paradise, to attend Baptist youth conferences across the country. It's challenging for me to fully explain the breadth of the lessons I learned at those youth conferences and the power those lessons still hold for me today, but I will do my best to share what I now understand is the very foundation of all that I have done and continue to do.

That said, this may sound crazy, but when I recollect that time, the memory that jumps most vividly to my mind is acting upon my first crush.

My girlfriends (many of whom were my cousins I grew up with) and I were excited for our first youth conference. The expectation of decorum and responsibility had been embedded in us, and we rose to the challenge, putting on our Sunday best clothes, making sure our hair was just right, and, most importantly, steadfastly listening to our elders and following the rules they had established. Standing in front of the church, next to a mountain of suitcases waiting to be loaded, we struggled to balance our urge to laugh and shout with excitement and our desire to act more grown up than we were as the large, gleaming charter buses pulled up in front of us and opened their doors, beckoning us in.

Standing just beyond the top of those steps, air conditioning swirling around me, and feeling the soft, cushy material as I placed my hand on top of a seat to steady myself and turn around to smile at my friends, I was breathless. I had never been on a bus that luxurious before. I'm not sure which one of us noticed first, but we were all stunned to find an actual bathroom in the back of the bus. A bathroom on a bus!

Once we made our way further down the aisle, we began giggling and whispering about which girls were going to sit next to which boys and which boys were smiling at us—all that awkward adolescent relationship dancing teenagers do. Down the aisle, all the way in the back, there sat my crush—alone. That set off a new round of giggles, and my girlfriends nudged me on, "Go sit with Shawn."

I could hardly contain my smile as I mustered up my courage and then threaded my way between the kids still standing in the aisle negotiating their own seating arrangements, hoping and praying all the way that no one would snatch that seat from me. I was a freshman in high school, and Shawn was a junior. At that age, a two-year gap is wide, and I'm sure Shawn thought of me as a younger sister type. But before I lost my nerve, I plopped myself down next to him, and he smiled at me and said, "Hi, Dee." I remember squealing to my girlfriends afterward, "He knew who I was!" Now, of course, with hindsight, I know that it would have been impossible for him not to know who I was. We all knew each other because we all spent every Sunday in church together and every Wednesday—and sometimes Saturdays—at youth activities together. Given the size of our church, you would have had to be invisible for everyone not to know who you were. But in that moment, on that bus, with hours of sitting side by side stretching ahead of us, Shawn's knowing who I was felt special and amazing. Over the next couple of days, I smiled at him and talked to him every chance I had, and that was enough of a connection for my naive thirteen-year-old self.

That was a big part of the beauty of those youth conferences: They provided us kids with a little bit of independence in an environment where we felt safe and supported and where our parents felt safe sending us. Yes, there were always adults present, many of whom I was related to, whether they were parents, aunts, uncles, or godparents. All of us had family connections that ran deep. And those who weren't family became an extension of our family through our shared experiences with and love for Paradise and our religious faith. But even within the confines of the bus, the chaperoning adults provided us space. They all sat up front together, giving us kids the rest of the bus to explore relationships with our peers in a different environment.

As amazing as riding the fancy bus and sitting next to my crush were, stepping into that first plenary session of the conference left me awestruck. It was in a huge, noisy space with rows upon rows of tables and a couple of thousand people huddling in small groups, chatting, lining up for their name tags and conference packages, or weaving in and out of the tables in search of a seat. At the front of the room was a large dais, and on top of it was a blur of motion as chairs, tables, microphones, and people were being adjusted for the opening session. I could feel my friend tugging on my arm to go, but I stood firmly planted, reveling in the wonder of it all: *What is this, how does this work, and who are these people?* I wanted answers to all of it.

All these years later, I couldn't tell you what the content of those plenary sessions or the many breakout workshops I attended was. What I can recall is the incredible sense of empowerment. The awe of the opportunity to serve at that important conference as a delegate for my church and as a participant in that gathering of teenagers from Baptist churches across the country and to do so in an environment that, again, felt so safe and supportive of who I was and what I could accomplish.

The conferences were run as professionally as any conference I've participated in as an adult. While it was tailored to teenagers, it was not trivialized for us in any way. We followed proper parliamentary procedures. We learned how to run a meeting, how to network, and how to confidently navigate a conference of magnitude. It was the start of feeling like we were part of something much bigger than ourselves, our families, and our own churches. Most of the churches represented at the conference were Black churches, but I don't know if we even thought about that at the time. What we understood was that we were all part of an association of churches and we were representing the youth of that association.

These experiences that my parents and my church exposed me to not only laid the foundation for how I carry myself in the professional world today; they also fueled the strategy nerd I was destined to become.

When I left that first conference, I was energized and full of ideas, and lucky for me, so was my friend, Sherice. Within minutes of the bus departing from the conference center for our return trip home, Sherice and I had our heads bent together, whispering and glancing from side to side as if we were sharing national secrets that no one else should hear. *What do we do with all this information?* was at the heart of our impassioned impromptu strategy session. Sherice was an usher like me, and at that conference, we had heard from ushers at other churches about how their systems worked—and we liked some of their ways better than the way our usher program worked. Some of them didn't wear gloves, and some of them had cool name tags. "How can we get our usher board to agree to do things differently?" we asked as we continued to strategize in hushed tones. If no one overheard us, we thought, no one could tell us no before we even hatched a plan.

The Sunday after we returned from the youth conference, all the kids who had attended it were called to the front of the congregation. One or two of the older youth were tasked with sharing a little bit about our experience and lessons from the conference, and all the adults cheered and clapped for us.

The following week, Sherice and I had our strategy mapped out, and we presented our requests to the usher board. We were denied. My granny and the other founding members, who oversaw the usher board, were very traditional, and they saw the changing of our gloves or our name tags as too drastic, and that was that. But I continued to ask questions, bring new ideas, and challenge the status quo based on what I learned and heard, and we were exhilarated by the few small wins we managed to garner along the way. This process would serve to teach me that it was more about the how than the what. *How do you lead, grow, and change?*

Growing up, I felt that Paradise was home to me. It was the first place I led. It was the first place I loved. Just as it was Granny's everything, it became my everything.

It wasn't until I became an adult that I understood the bigger role that churches play in the Black community and the impact they have on how I continue to move through the world. As I look back and think about some of the women and men who were in various leadership roles in the church, I now understand they were leaders outside of the church too—in their jobs and in political and community roles. They modeled commitment, responsibility, and leadership and encouraged us to do the same. Black churches serve as political entities. They are often the core and the heartbeat of our communities. Black community, state, and national leaders visit churches like Paradise to inform their members of the issues inside and outside of their own communities and show them how to mobilize for a cause. Our churches provide the foundation on which faith, family, and community are built. My family was raised on that foundation.

It was a foundation that taught me that everyone matters and that everyone should have equal access to opportunities. It is that foundation upon which I have built my leadership career.

CHAPTER 3

MY SHOT

"My Shot"

Hey yo, I'm just like my country
I'm young, scrappy and hungry
And I'm not throwing away my shot

—from *Hamilton: An American Musical*

hen I was in middle school, I said that I was going to be a doctor. Doctors were smart, they were leaders in their communities, and they helped people; those were qualities I aspired to. Then I learned what a medical doctor did, and I decided that wasn't for me. Then I figured out that there were other kinds of doctors, and I knew that I was going to become one of those kinds of doctors. I had been in gifted programs since first grade, and I had always been that student who took advantage of every opportunity. When I decided I was going to pursue a PhD, my motivation accelerated.

The summer before I was to begin high school, I attended a six-week summer academic enrichment program at Archbishop O'Hara Catholic High School with my best friend, Marshaun, whom I had met the previous year when I transferred into the middle school she was attending. There, we would meet our new lifelong best friend, Kisa.

It was our next-level passion for learning that drew us together. This summer enrichment program recruited the best and brightest eighth-grade students from the inner-city Catholic middle schools and exposed them to O'Hara's teachers and curriculum, which included advanced placement (AP) classes that were not as readily offered as they are today. O'Hara was a predominately white, suburban Catholic high school, and the inner-city Catholic high school was predominately Black.

I remember first meeting Kisa when we worked together on a newspaper project, reporting on everything we learned during the program. Kisa was as passionate and confident as I was, never shy about voicing her perspective, and always meticulous about her research that informed her perspective. I thought, *She's just like me!* with her no-nonsense, let's-get-on-with-it style. The perfect balance to our bumpy edges came in Marshaun, whose soft and welcoming nature always ensured everyone was included and everyone's voice was heard and who never had a negative word to say about anyone. Together, we were, and still are, the perfect balance for each other.

Through that enrichment program, I recognized that O'Hara would provide me with the level of academics that I knew would set me on the path to a PhD. What I couldn't have foreseen was that the three of us would become lifelong supporters on each other's journeys. In the fall of 1988, Marshaun and I began our freshman year at O'Hara while Kisa enrolled at the Catholic school in the inner city. Despite attending different high schools, we maintained our connection through shared participation in various external programs and internships.

This bond held firm even as our college journeys diverged: Kisa and Marshaun attended historically Black colleges and universities in Tennessee while I headed off to the West Coast for school. Today, our lives reflect that enduring connection and the impact of our early aspirations. Marshaun is now the chief operating officer for a major health system in Kansas City, and Kisa is a senior electrical engineer and project manager for a leading architecture, engineering, and construction (AEC) company. Their contributions extend beyond their professions; both are well known for their service on civic boards and have received numerous awards for their civic contributions. We continue to strengthen and encourage one another because, at our core, we are the same.

It's remarkable that we found each other so early in life, before we fully understood how closely our values, our faith, or our trajectories would align. Yet, we saw something special in each other, and that connection has never faded. A connection that began in the halls of O'Hara that summer so many years ago—halls that would indeed shape so much more of my journey in unexpected ways.

From the moment I stepped through the doors of Archbishop O'Hara Catholic High School as a freshman until the day of my graduation, I applied for and was active in high school leadership programs and conferences. I was in student government, and in my sophomore year, I was nominated by my high school to be our representative at the Hugh O'Brian Youth Leadership (HOBY) state conference. This opportunity would truly change my life.

HOBY is a youth leadership organization that develops and inspires youth around the globe to become outstanding, lifelong leaders. The four-day conference was held on a college campus. I was surrounded by sophomores from all over Missouri, and we stayed in the dorms and went through all the leadership training together. I found myself sitting shoulder to shoulder in a room filled with motivated, excited, and inspiring high school sophomores who were just as nerdy as me. For the first time, I wasn't the only kid chasing leadership conferences and summer opportunities. I wasn't the only kid driven to do more and go more places. I remember breaking into small groups and competing to develop a product idea or come up with a solution for a societal issue. We were young teenagers, but we talked about important things, and our counselors listened.

At night, after we ended our leadership sessions, we would sit around in big circles, sing songs, and share what we worried about, what we cared about, what we wanted to strive for, and what we wanted to achieve. And nobody made fun. That was the difference. Nobody believed your thoughts or ideas were stupid. It was the first place in which I didn't feel like I had to temper what I said because, here, everyone's thoughts and ideas were just as outrageous as mine. I finally fit in.

At HOBY, I found people who helped me dream big things for myself academically. Throughout the remainder of high school, I would be very involved in HOBY while continuing to participate in activities at O'Hara. In my senior year, two pivotal experiences would lead me to my life's work. The first was an incident upon which racial lines were drawn, and the second was the process of applying to colleges.

O'Hara was a predominately white school. The Black students made up less than 10 percent of the student body of O'Hara, and many of us were bussed in from the inner city. All the other students either lived close enough to walk to school or were driven by their parents. In the middle of my senior year, our basketball team was badly beaten in one of the final games, knocking it out of contention for whatever the next level of the season was. The school that beat it so badly was a predominately Black school from one of the inner-city public schools. O'Hara hosted the game, and the result didn't sit well.

Later that night, our school was vandalized. The following morning, when word spread that it was the winning team who were the vandals, fights began to break out between the Black and white students in our school. For O'Hara's Black students, it just didn't ring true that the winning team (the predominately Black team) had done the vandalizing because what the vandals wrote on our school bus—the bus that transported the Black and Latino kids (something only the O'Hara students knew)—wasn't what Black players would have written.

The vandals wrote things such as "soul train" and "niggers go home." Those were not terms that Black students would use to vandalize a predominately white school. But when you're white and privileged ...

It just didn't add up. Tensions escalated, and fights broke out in the hallways and classrooms. People screamed and ran through the building, and the fire doors caught, locking us in the hallways. I remember trying to figure out what was going on and trying to talk to the administration, but they weren't listening to me. I was frustrated that they wouldn't listen—I couldn't understand why they wouldn't listen. My boyfriend, Kelly, was not trying to figure it out. He was in the thick of the scuffle, fighting and running through the school. How differently Kelly and I interacted with the world around us would become a thread woven through many chapters of my life.

Our school was in the middle of a mini race riot, and the school administration decided the best way to handle it was to usher all the Black students into the auditorium and insist we remain there for the rest of the school day. Two other students and I managed to sneak out (we were the "good kids," so no one worried about us) and call our parents from the pay phones just outside the door. When our parents and the parents of the other Black students came to the school, everything exploded.

Our parents were outraged that they had separated us, and the all-white administration countered that they thought they were doing the right thing by keeping us safe. I knew it then, and I know it now: We should not have been removed from our classrooms. We shouldn't have.

I want to step back for a moment. At that point in time, I was in my senior year. Black students represented about 10 percent of the student population, but we felt like we were part of the fabric of O'Hara life. What I mean by that is that we had friends of all colors and backgrounds. We served on the student council, and we led organizations. We were even cheerleaders—Marshaun, my friend Christie, and I. In our senior year, Marshaun was the homecoming queen, I was the court warming queen, and our friend Marla was the prom queen. There was a local article about us, "Three Friends, Three Queens." I was salutatorian. The Black students, while only 10 percent of the student body, were integral to the school and all its activities. I share all this to say that I never felt any sense of separateness or divisiveness along racial lines during my four years there.

That is why the eruption of that mini race riot was so unexpected and so shocking for all of us—students, faculty, administration, and parents. Or maybe not our parents.

Our parents collected us from the auditorium that day. In the days immediately following, the parents of the Black students demanded answers to why the administration separated their kids, locked them in the auditorium, and refused to let them out. They demanded that the administration talk about it, and they demanded to know how they were addressing what happened.

I can't recall the exact timeline, but within about a week of the incident, there was a sit-down with the Black students and their families and the administration and faculty. Walking into the school that evening, alongside my parents and the other parents and students, the anger and anxiety we all felt sat heavily on our collective shoulders as we pushed open the big double doors of the library and entered the large, square room with the last rays of daylight streaming through its huge glass windows. Before us were heavy wooden tables lined up to form one long row through the center of the room. Once we were all settled and our principal began to speak from his seat at the far end of the table, it struck me how impossible it was for the thirty-five to forty people seated around this single line of tables to even see each other.

That would be an initial indication of how the meeting would progress. The principal started the meeting by recapping what had happened and why it had happened. He didn't open up space for questions, but the parents had plenty, and tempers began to flare.

There was a lot of crying, particularly by the students. We, too, were active participants in this meeting, and several students shared how it felt to be locked in the auditorium all day, having to sneak out to the pay phones in the hall to call our parents because the administration did not allow us to freely do so. Being forced to remain there while we could hear screaming and yelling and fights busting out in the hallway was distressing for all of us. The most-expressed sentiment by the students at that meeting was, "You're supposed to protect us, but instead, you locked us up."

I don't recall any sense of resolution when that meeting ended or any significant changes in the days and weeks that followed. I do remember side conversations with teachers who would stop us, particularly if there was a group of us Black students together, and ask if we were doing OK. Our cheerleading coach, Mrs. South, did check in with the entire cheer team after the incident, asking how we were all doing and providing us with space to express ourselves.

As heightened as my emotions were during and immediately following the incident, within days after the meeting with the administration, I honestly checked out. I was graduating from high school in a couple of weeks and then heading off to college in the fall. That was my solitary focus, and I no longer gave a damn about what happened at O'Hara. Nothing since the incident had changed among my core group of high school friends, Black and white. I don't even remember having any real conversations among ourselves about the riot and its fallout. Maybe that was because we were all seniors, had been together for four years, and already had one foot out the door. Or maybe it was just me compartmentalizing—a coping mechanism I wouldn't recognize until much later in life, by which point I had unconsciously mastered it.

That's not to suggest I wasn't impacted; I was. The incident was the first time that I had been faced with pure racism. I remember struggling to understand why everyone wasn't equally outraged by what had happened. I'm a thinker, and so, in that moment, when race and discrimination became emotionally charged for me, I thought, *No, no, no, there must be a better way to deal with this. Yelling, fighting, and being locked in an auditorium are not the way. Neither is allowing the situation to continue to exist without talking about it or trying to fix it.* Even though I didn't have the words at the time, it was my first recognition that what happened was not the outlier I initially felt it to be; it was a symptom of a larger, systemic crisis.

Moving forward from this experience, I intentionally sought out the words, the language, and the skills to not just exist with issues of race and discrimination but to heal from them, learn from them, and eventually teach them.

The second pivotal thing that occurred during my senior year was the process of applying to colleges. HOBY played a critical role in that process.

At HOBY, I had a junior counselor named Sarah. She was a young Latina college student from Kansas City, Missouri. Over the next year, as I trained to be a junior counselor and got more involved with HOBY, we became great friends. One day, while we were talking, it dawned on me that Sarah was Black and Brown, like me. Sarah was from the inner city, like me. Sarah was a student at Cornell University ... did that mean I could be a student at Cornell University? I began to look at the sphere of potential colleges and universities differently. I was at a Catholic high school, so the counselors pushed places like the University of Notre Dame for those of us who were the top scholars. Notre Dame was at the top of my list initially. By the time I began applying, Notre Dame was listed below Georgetown University, the University of Southern California (USC), Stanford University, and Cornell. I also applied to the University of Missouri (MU) because my daddy asked me to in hopes that I would remain close to home. I didn't understand it then, but I truly understand it now as a mother to a high school student.

My application to MU was the one my high school counselor made sure I got in on time. We were reviewing my college list, and she said to me, "You are one of our best and brightest, and I don't want you to be in a situation where you do not have an amazing option. I know you'll get into MU, and I know that you will receive multiple scholarships, if not a full ride." And while I believe she said it from a place of support, in that moment, what I heard was, "Little Black girl, you're overreaching. These elite schools are beyond you." Those moments were hard, and they were also what fueled my fire—*I'll show you,* I thought.

Even though I was gifted, I still noticed subtle messages in school questioning whether I was good enough. I remember fighting to get into honors math as a freshman because someone looked at my high school entrance scores and determined that my high scores must have been a fluke and that I was not ready for honors math. Being underestimated was nothing new, and it has continued to be a source of motivation to this day.

I graduated second in my high school class—the first ever Black salutatorian in the history of the school. The lowest grade on my entire high school transcript was an A–, and most of my classes were AP and honors. In my senior year, I was part of an extremely small cohort of students who had blown so far past the math curriculum that a teacher from one of the local colleges was brought in to teach us AP Calculus BC on the side. I was a HOBY alum. I was meant to reach as high as possible, and nobody, well-meaning or not, was going to make me believe otherwise.

USC, Cornell, Notre Dame, and Georgetown were among the first to send me acceptance letters. Georgetown had the School of Foreign Service and a substantial international program. I was like, *boom, this is it.* Then I received a big envelope with bold Cardinal red letters that said "YES STANFORD!" You didn't even have to open that puppy up to know you got in. I remember sort of half-reading the letter, and then I saw a handwritten note from the dean of admission.

One of Stanford's traditions is that the dean handwrites a note on the bottom of every admission letter. At the time, the dean was James Montoya, who would later become a mentor to me. The college essay I submitted was about how my grandparents didn't have high school diplomas, and my parents didn't have college degrees, but it was because I could stand on their shoulders that I was able to do the work that brought me to that point. The handwritten note on my admission letter from Dean Montoya was, "I know that those shoulders are proud of you."

That's when I knew that Stanford was the place I wanted to be. At Stanford, I wouldn't just be a number. I wouldn't just be the Black girl from Kansas City, an affirmative action admittance. They had read my essay, and they had seen me.

I showed all my acceptance letters to my school counselor. When I showed her my acceptance into Stanford, I said, "Now maybe some of those other kids that you wanted to get into Notre Dame can take the spot that I released." I've always been a little sassy, but that's how I felt. I worked hard. I was at the top of my class, and when I said, "I want to apply to Stanford, Cornell, and Georgetown," it was her sole job to double down and figure out how to help me reach for my dreams. For so many Black students, it is that person in authority and power who tells them it's not possible that stops them from submitting that application and reaching for their dreams.

Although I didn't fully grasp it at the time, these experiences served as the springboard to my life's work: creating access and opportunity for all.

At the time, I didn't know what it would take financially to get myself to Stanford, but people told me that, if I worked hard as a student and got good grades, schools would provide me with scholarships. Stanford does not give out merit scholarships; all their financial aid is based on need. My parents' middle-income level meant my financial aid package included the expectation that my parents would pay a hefty share of my college tuition—dollar amounts larger than their annual mortgage, dollar amounts they simply did not have.

The reality was that if I was going to attend and graduate from Stanford, no matter how much I excelled academically, I had to figure out a way to pay for it. I spent my high school summers working at

Worlds of Fun, an amusement park in Kansas City, Missouri, saving every penny I could for school. I also applied for every scholarship and financial award I could find. I was racking up as many $250 and $500 scholarships as possible. Award ceremony after award ceremony, my dad would always be with me, and he'd say, "How do you even find this stuff?" I rarely won the top local or regional awards. They often went to students attending MU or the University of Kansas (KU), and I came in second or third.

My dad tells the story of sitting at the ceremonies with the other parents and being the only Black family at the table and often one of the only Black families in the room. After the first and second place awards won by the MU and KU students were announced, my third place award and school would be announced. The white parents would look at him like he had two heads and horns, as if to say, *How can your daughter be going to Stanford?* But that was our journey. Between my parents' financial assistance and my scholarships, savings, and student loans, I entered my freshman year at Leland Stanford Junior University in the fall of 1992.

While I was not the first grandchild in my family to go off to college, I was going to be the farthest and the only one who needed to fly to get from school to home. If you remember the signature anchor stores of yesterday, you remember The Jones Store Co. It was the premier place to shop, which we only went to on very special occasions. At Granny's request, Mom picked her up and drove us to The Jones Store Co. one Saturday morning. Granny looked at me and said, "You need a new set of luggage for that fancy school so far away." She bought me my own set of matching blue-and-pink floral six-piece luggage set. It was her way of saying she was proud but also reminding me to "bring my tail back home!"

CHAPTER 4
SPECIAL

"Special"

In case nobody told you today, You're special
In case nobody made you believe, You're special
I will always love you the same, You're special

—Lizzo

s undergraduates, especially in those first few years, many of us wander around trying to figure out what we're doing, where we want to go, and how we're going to get there. Thankfully, for many of us at Stanford, we found a guiding light, Mama Jewel. Or more accurately, she found us.

Jewel Boswell Hudson's office was just inside the door of Tresidder Memorial Union, Stanford's student union. Tresidder houses Stanford's student government, the Associated Students of Stanford University. The first time I walked up the front stairs and into its grand entrance hall filled with light streaming in from the massive glass panels all along the front of the building, I knew this was a place of significance. This was the hub of student affairs, with meeting spaces, study areas, computer labs, a coffeehouse, tables inside and out, a bike shop, a copy center, and the legal aid office, run by Mama Jewel. If a student needed free legal aid, it was Mama Jewel's job to arrange for lawyers outside of Stanford to assist them pro bono. But I would quickly learn that Mama Jewel's love for her students reached far beyond the scope of her job description.

One day, in my freshman year, I walked into the student union hoping to find information about job openings. I had only made it a few feet into the hall when I heard a voice call, "Baby, what you need?"

"Me?" I asked, turning to the sound of the voice and landing my eyes on a petite woman emerging from behind her desk with a smile so wide it reached her big round eyes.

"Yes, you," she said, waving me over. "Come here, baby." She pointed me to one of the chairs in front of her desk and then sat down in the one next to it. "Now," she said, "tell me what you need."

I explained to her that I was struggling financially, and I needed a job. We talked a little bit about what I could do, and then she stood up and said, "Come with me," and off we went to the lecture notes and copy center just two doors down from Mama Jewel's office. Mama Jewel introduced me to Kristi Hillman and then asked Kristi, "Y'all hiring? 'Cause y'all should hire DeAngela, here."

And that was how I landed my first job at Stanford and how I met Kristi, who would become one of my dearest friends. Kristi was a junior at the time, and I was fortunate to work with her at the center until her graduation the following year, after which she returned to her home state of Washington. Though geographically, the distance between us grew significantly, our friendship remained close. Several years later, Kristi would be in my wedding, and we would continue to play important roles in each other's lives. Kristi is one of the many gifts Mama Jewel bestowed on me.

It didn't take us students long to understand the power of Mama Jewel—if any student had a need (even if they didn't know what that need was yet), she helped them fill it. As warm, funny, and kind as Mama Jewel was, she was also tough. If you didn't follow through, if you didn't do what you were supposed to be doing, she'd get right to the point. "Why didn't you take care of that?" she'd ask, *and* she'd expect an answer. The next question would be, "How are you going to fix this?" She'd support you through the steps you needed to take to fix it, but she wouldn't fix it for you. Mama Jewel taught us the importance of being accountable for our actions.

For me, Mama Jewel felt like home. Her big smile, deep and hearty laugh, and smooth, caramel-colored skin reminded me of Granny. Mama Jewel was a safe port for me to return to time and time again as I navigated student life at Stanford. It was Mama Jewel who, just a few months later, helped me land my second job at Stanford when she introduced me to another amazing Black woman, Jeanette Smith-Laws. Like Mama Jewel, Jeanette has helped so many struggling students over the years, giving us jobs at the Student Union in which we would walk around locking and unlocking doors and locking up the building at the end of the day. That's all we did, which meant we could sit in that quiet space and study while we waited to unlock the next door.

Jeanette understood our needs and helped fill them. She will tell you, "I employed all of them. Every last one." We are her Stanford babies, and she reminds us at every reunion that she gave us our first real jobs. Stanford was filled with these beautiful people and, particularly for me, beautiful Black leaders.

During my senior year, when I began work on my honors thesis, Mama Jewel once again significantly impacted my Stanford experience and beyond. But first, let me share how the topic of my honors thesis came to be.

I entered Stanford undecided, but I knew early in high school that I wanted to study international policy. What I didn't know when I entered Stanford was that I would also choose African American studies. Stanford, as a community and an institution, provided me with the environment to begin to articulate what I was feeling, what I was doing, and what I wanted to understand about race and discrimination. When I found African American studies, I found the words, the language, and the skills that had eluded me in high school to develop the expertise to not just exist with issues and challenges of race but to understand them, to learn from them, to teach them, to deal with them, and to heal from them.

When I told my dad that I wanted to major in African American studies, he said, "You're going to Stanford to learn about Black people? You want to learn about Black people? You can walk down the street; you can talk to your cousins. Black people are all around you. You Black, right?"

"This is more than knowing Black people, Daddy," I said, "This is history and developing the understanding and skills to make things better." I told him about my professor, Clayborne Carson, whom Coretta Scott King appointed director of the Martin Luther King, Jr. Papers Project. "I'm doing research with Dr. King's notes, his actual notes, Daddy," I told him excitedly. I think in the end, he understood, but the fact that I didn't drop my international relations major made it OK for me to also study Black people.

I chose to do an honors thesis research project (that's the only way a student can graduate with honors from Stanford) that was a marriage of my dual degrees in international relations and African/African American studies. My thesis topic was the African American influence on US foreign policy toward Africa. I honored my African American studies throughout my academic career. They weren't secondary to me; they were prominent. It was through my studies at Stanford and Stanford's culture that I realized I didn't have to choose between being Black and being an intellectual. They were one and the same. Being a Black woman is a part of the excellence that I bring to the table. It's not separate. It is integrated. From that point forward, I chose to move through my life as a proud Black woman of excellence.

When I shared my thesis concept with Mama Jewel, she sat me down and said, "Well, let me tell you about my time in Oakland." The woman who chose to not only see me but to help me in so many ways had been a leader in the Black Panther Party! This wonderful Black woman, who was a leader at Stanford University, had been—and in many ways, still was in 1995—a revolutionary. Mama Jewel was no longer a member of the Black Panther Party, but she still had passion and fire to help build the next generation of Black leaders.

Mama Jewel knew and understood the power of who we would be in the world and the promise we would bring to our communities. There are pivotal people in your life, and then there are the Mama Jewels whose importance words cannot explain. They are the ones who inspire us to be better and to do better every day. In 2017, twenty-five years after I first met Mama Jewel, she met my then–nine-year-old son, Xavier, for the first time, and he would call her Moo Moo Jewel from that point forward. I would come to appreciate these full circle moments in my life.

I have been blessed to have so many people who chose to come into my life with the only goal of helping me. My family and friends have always been supportive of me, even when my drive and dreams were different from theirs. Growing up in Kansas City, I always wanted to do more, to see more, and to learn everything. My family will tell people, "Yeah, DeAngela's different. She's always been like that." But no matter where my dreams take me, they are there, supporting me 100 percent.

When those dreams took me to Stanford and gave me the opportunity to be the first person in my immediate family to graduate from college, my parents, brother, and godparents were by my side the first time I drove onto Stanford's campus. The first time was at the commencement of freshman move-in day and the week of orientation that followed. You see, I had applied for and accepted my spot at Stanford sight unseen. As I think back on that fact, it seemed a bit crazy, but the reality was that it was perfect.

I can remember my feelings of giddy excitement and a bit of nervousness as we stood at the Kansas City International Airport baggage check-in, passing over suitcase after suitcase after suitcase, hoping the airport staff wouldn't turn any of them away. My mom, dad, brother, and godparents had at least one bag each that was really a bag of my stuff. Stanford was not a drivable distance from home, so I needed the contents of each of those suitcases to fly there with me!

My skin still tingles when I recall that first instant I entered Stanford's campus. As my father turned our rental car onto Stanford's iconic Palm Drive, I quickly rolled down my window and leaned my head out, craning to see the tops of the majestic palm trees lining both sides of the one-mile entranceway. I am confident that I squealed with excitement that I could not contain—and probably more than once. "I can't believe I'm here!" was what I wanted to shout into the warm California breeze—but my mom would have been appalled if I had. Shouting out of windows was not proper, and we didn't want these people to think I didn't know how to act. And then, without warning, I was suddenly awed into silence as Stanford's architectural crown jewel, Stanford Memorial Church, came into view. When I tell you I could hear angels singing, I could hear angels singing. It remains, to this day, one of the most beautiful visions I have ever laid eyes on. That I, DeAngela Burns, a young Black woman from Kansas City, Missouri, was going to school there felt at once surreal and unequivocally exactly where I was meant to be.

And then all too quickly, it was time to get to work moving in. My parents and Jason helped me haul all my stuff to the dorm, unpack my suitcases, and get my room all set up. Doing so required multiple runs to Target (which didn't exist in Missouri at the time) for all the essentials I didn't know I needed. My roommate's parents knew how to set up a room, and we tried to follow their lead. My freshman roommate, also a young Black woman, was named Angela—yes, we joked that someone in housing had fun pairing two Black females named Angela and DeAngela together. Angela and her family already knew Stanford as her brother had just graduated the year before. They would be a guide for us not only for simply things like setting up that first dorm room but throughout my first year.

What I would come to learn about having a roommate, and about the beauty of the entire college experience, was that it immersed me in new ideas, thoughts, and experiences. Not just roommates, Angela and I became good friends that shared simple things and more deeper ones too. The simple ones, like music—while Angela liked Boyz II Men, she got tired of hearing "End of the Road" on repeat every single night while trying to sleep, it became our running joke. But Angela introduced me to new artists like Toad the Wet Sprocket, who played at our freshman welcome concert—music I would have never chosen on my own. It may sound simple, but I appreciated Angela showing me different things and just being there for me that year. Throughout our time at Stanford, we would check in, show up for each other, cheer each other on over and over again. My first Stanford relationship became a special part of my journey. At Black graduation in our senior year, we were in line to get our Kente cloths from our parents, standing side by side just as we were when we started our Stanford journey together. Over the years we have followed each other's careers and personal journeys, cheering each other on at milestones like our children, degrees, and more. We still have the Angela–DeAngela connection but now it's Dr. Angela/Dr. DeAngela—someone in housing knew something we didn't and I'm forever grateful.

Going back to the beginning, the funniest part of moving in was that our dormmates kept coming out of their rooms and into ours to introduce themselves. My neighbors on both sides popped in, saying, "I'm next door." At some point, my dad looked at me and asked, "Why are there only boys coming in here telling me that they live next door?"

"Oh, Daddy," I explained, "All the dorms are coed." He was not impressed. Later, during orientation, he found out that I had the choice of an all-girls floor or a coed floor and made sure to let me know that my choices probably weren't the best. My dad would also never get used to men answering the telephone in my room, even though I wasn't even in my room when they did so. Because we were in a small freshman dorm, we would leave our doors open when we left our rooms but were still somewhere in the building, and often we would answer our neighbors' phones if we were around. My dad got to know Dave Conti, my neighbor, well because Dave usually answered the phone when I wasn't there. It would throw my dad every time.

My parents, brother, and godparents attended convocation with me. Together, we sat in the Main Quad, regarded as the heart of Stanford's campus. Its wide, open archway provided us with a view once again of Stanford's spectacular Memorial Church. As the dean of admission welcomed our class, I remember sitting there, breathing in the beauty of Stanford with my family sitting next to me, and thinking, *This is where I was supposed to be all my life.* I felt no fear of what was next or of my parents leaving me there. What I felt most was energized. I couldn't wait to start doing all the stuff I knew I was meant to do.

That orientation week, there were parent activities and student activities, and my parents spent considerable time on campus meeting faculty and administrators, attending parent receptions, and learning about the Stanford experience. By Friday of freshman orientation week, most parents had departed, but my parents, brother, and godparents stayed the weekend. We went to San Francisco and did all the tourist things, such as visiting Fisherman's Wharf and Alcatraz, just soaking in as much as we could.

As they were getting ready to head home, my dad said, "I've talked to these people, to some of these students and teachers. You fit here, DeAngela. You found your people." For my dad to understand that, outside of the love and support of my family, this was the first place that I truly felt like I fit in, that people understood me just as I was, meant everything to me.

While HOBY had given me that first taste, whenever I left a HOBY event and came back to my school and my community, I felt even more different. I didn't need to leave Stanford; I was there to stay.

One of the most powerful things I learned at Stanford was that I didn't have to choose between being Black and being smart because at Stanford, we weren't seen as needing to be one or the other. We all had these crazy ideas, and we all wanted to change the world. When I said I was going to run Disney one day, people were like, "OK, let's see how we get you there, Dee. Let's see who we know." At Stanford, nobody thought I was too much. It was an environment filled with Marshauns and Kisas—people I could be myself with. People who didn't think I was pushing too hard or asking too many questions. People around whom I didn't feel the need to tone myself down.

Stanford was my game changer. Not solely because I'd get a good education that would lead to a good job, but because it would change my mindset. And not just mine; it changed the mindset of the people in my community and in my family. I was creating ripples for the girls and boys who would follow my path and find their Stanford—wherever that might be.

I am the product of the power of an environment like Stanford for a young Black girl from Kansas City. To know that power and to know there are so many kids and families to whom no one ever said, "You could go there. Why not you?" is to know that I must be a catalyst. I must be a part of ensuring that an institution that is committed to creating access, and believes in cultivating rich diversity with that access, does it well and does it continuously. That is why Stanford is so critical to me, why I have been an active alum, and why I now serve on the board of trustees.

I continued working at the local amusement park, Worlds of Fun, the summer after my freshman year at Stanford, and by my sophomore year, I wasn't sure how I was going to be able to continue paying my tuition. Working two, sometimes three, jobs just wasn't enough to fill the gap left by my student loans, but I was determined. My solution came as a dinner invitation. As a sophomore, I was invited to a fancy dinner at the Faculty Club for emerging sophomore scholars of color. I didn't even know what that meant at the time. All I knew was that I would get a free meal, and it would be fun to dress up. That evening, sitting at that round table with a white linen tablecloth, Cardinal red–colored napkins, and a full place setting that I wasn't even sure how to use, a faculty member, Dr. Kennell Jackson, changed my life. That dinner would always stay with me, and years later, it would become another full circle moment that I would savor.

But on that winter evening in 1994, it was my introduction to undergraduate fellowships—programs sponsored by a specific association, organization, institution, or government agency that focused on professional, academic, and/or personal development—that would set the trajectory of my career in motion.

The head of Stanford's Office of Undergraduate Research at the time created a fellowship night for sophomores of color who had a certain GPA to meet with faculty members and with upperclassmen who were currently participating in fellowships. This event introduced us to the concept of what fellowships were, what undergraduate research was, how these things came together, and, most importantly, how to access the money to do all of these things and more.

I did my research after that night. In 1994, that research found me sitting cross-legged on the floor in a conference room in Sweet Hall, surrounded by file folders. The walls of the room were lined with large, metal lateral files, and it was in those drawers that I sorted through fellowship options. This was all new to me, but eventually I discovered that there existed fellowships related to studies in public policy. And as I began to look through those applications, I realized that they weren't much different from all those scholarship applications I had completed in high school, and I began to find familiar ground.

I learned that fellowships not only provided money in the form of scholarships but also through paid internships or other experiences. They also provided the structure I needed to help me figure out my path. I had the edges of a plan. I knew I wanted to do something in the international arena, and I had known for a few years by then that I wanted to get my doctorate, but I hadn't figured out just how to make that all happen. I applied to about ten fellowships, and the one I most wanted was the Coca-Cola Olympics Fellowship.

The Olympics were coming to Atlanta in 1996, and this fellowship would allow me to work with an Olympic national team and travel a couple of times a year to their country to meet with them. I was an international relations major, I was taking French, and I was preparing to study overseas at Stanford's campus in Paris, and so, to me, this was the ideal fellowship. It would provide some scholarship money, a paid internship in the summers, and then in my senior year, I would get to be a part of the Olympics as a team interpreter.

I was a finalist for the Coca-Cola, Mellon, and Pickering fellowships. I hadn't given much thought to what the Pickering Fellowship offered because, in my mind, I was going to the Olympics! So when the call came inviting me to DC to interview as a Pickering finalist, I was excited but not nervous—that was, until I understood the magnitude of its financial impact.

Pickering flew their twenty finalists to DC and put us up in a fancy hotel (with the biggest tub I had ever seen—and yes, I enjoyed a bubble bath in it) across from the State Department. I remember that on the night I arrived in DC, I tried to learn as much about the fellowship as possible. But it was a new program, and the cohort they were interviewing then would only be its third, so there was little for me to research. What I knew was that the Foreign Service fellowship opportunity dovetailed well with my international relations major and that only ten of us would be accepted. That same night, my dad called to remind me to get something to eat, get to bed early, and make sure I set my alarm. That was my dad's thing: You got to eat, you got to sleep, and don't be late!

Walking into the State Department, I experienced the same awe and energy that had stopped me in my tracks when I had stepped into my first plenary session as a member of Paradise's youth group. The grand lobby through which we entered the State Department was a massive space—three stories high, with floor-to-ceiling windows and gleaming marble floors. High above, uniformly posted along the lobby's top edges, were vibrantly colored flags representing countries from around the globe. I was many things in that moment—awestruck, most definitely. But also simultaneously overwhelmed and exhilarated by the grandeur and tradition of it all. Just like when I entered Stanford's campus, I knew that I was meant to be there.

Over the next two days, the Pickering representatives introduced us to the Foreign Service and the depth of the financial support of the fellowship (they would pay for the last two years of our undergraduate degrees *and* graduate school 100 percent), and they put each of us through a grueling interview process. We sat before a panel of Foreign Service diplomats, who shot rapid-fire questions at us and expected proper responses. Dr. Richard Hope (the director of the fellowship) and Ambassador Ruth A. Davis, who would become lifelong mentors for me, were members of the panel. When Dr. Hope asked me why I was interested in this fellowship, I said, "I'm out of money, and this scholarship will take me through grad school." He laughed at my candor and teased me for years afterward about how I was the only one who gave such an honest, no-nonsense answer.

When I understood the impact Pickering could have on my future, that was when I became nervous—nervous that I wouldn't be chosen. When a first-generation kid like me, who's scraping together scholarships and working two or three jobs in hopes that it will cover the cost of tuition, is told that someone is willing to pay for their last two years of undergrad *and* grad school 100 percent, they jump at it with few questions asked. And when I got the call on early Monday morning and heard the words, "I want to congratulate you on being selected as a

State Department fellow," I absolutely jumped—and maybe screamed a bit, which woke up my roommate, Leyda, who jumped and screamed with me. Then I called my parents. Now my parents are not jumpers and screamers like me; I am the least reserved member of my family. My parents congratulated me and then wanted to know what it all meant for my schooling and future and what the next steps were.

My next step was signing the Pickering Fellowship contract. It arrived the following week in what was the thickest and most intimidating FedEx envelope I had ever seen. Without hesitation, I brought it to Mama Jewel. She talked me through it, and when we finished, she folded her hands, looked at me all serious, and said, "You understand, baby, once you sign this, you are bound to Foreign Service work for ten years."

Again, I was a nineteen-year-old, first-generation college kid whose finances were drying up. The truth was that if this scholarship with the Foreign Service had required me to walk down the street and pick my toes every day in between my Foreign Service work, I probably still would have said yes because all I saw in that moment was a clear path that would lead me to my doctorate and the ability to change the world in all the ways I envisioned.

For me, making that commitment turned out to be an incredible opportunity—as it did for many others. But in later years, I would advise new fellows in a way that ensured they fully comprehended the long-term commitment. Significant life changes occur between the ages of nineteen and twenty-nine—opportunities and challenges impossible to anticipate—necessitating that fellows thoroughly understand the commitment they are making.

The Pickering Fellowship, the Foreign Service, and, most especially, Ambassador Ruth A. Davis would have a profound impact on who I would become and how I would learn to lead.

CHAPTER 5

THE JOURNEY

"The Journey"

All the times they thought that they could hold you back
But you've always known there was no chance of that
You're made (you're made) too strong (too strong)

—H.E.R.

hen US Ambassador Ruth A. Davis walked into the room and called your name, you snapped to attention. A tall Black woman with a tight salt-and-pepper afro, Ambassador Davis had a commanding presence. She was someone I could see myself in, and upon first meeting her, I aspired to one day command that same type of presence. It was the Pickering Fellowship, originally called the Foreign Affairs Fellowship, that connected me to Ambassador Davis. She, Dr. Richard Hope, and several Black ambassadors and senior Foreign Service officers intentionally and strategically worked to diversify the Foreign Service through the Pickering Fellowship that first began in 1992.

The goal was to find the best and the brightest students of color across the nation, teach them how to be professional diplomats, and equip them with resources to gain access and opportunity to spaces and places that were historically closed off to them. They provided us with senior representatives who looked like us and who became the role models of excellence that we would strive to be.

When I began the program in 1994, I was one of only thirty recipients from across the nation. Even now, thirty years later and with close to a thousand Pickering alumni, I still have access to my incredible early mentors, who continue to break down barriers for the underrepresented. I am proud to be one ripple in their leadership journey, to be someone they opened doors for—doors that I didn't even know existed. It was the financial, educational, and mentor support of the Pickering Fellowship that enabled me to graduate from Stanford, immediately jump into a master's program at Princeton University, and graduate from two top-tier institutions with minimal college debt.

I graduated from Stanford in the spring of 1996, and that fall, I entered Princeton as a graduate student. But before I headed to Princeton, I spent the summer of 1996 at my first post as a Pickering intern. I was assigned to the United Nations (UN) desk in Washington, DC. The DC office supported the UN headquarters in New York. All UN issues came through the DC office, and we did all their background work. We even drafted resolutions for the UN headquarters, which is what happened when I was at the desk and we got a call. Not a standard "I'm so-and-so with such-and-such" call but a rapid-fire, one-way conversation about a coup happening in that moment in the Republic of Burundi, located in Sub-Saharan Africa. I scribbled notes down as fast as I could. I remember hanging up the phone, looking around, and thinking, *There's a coup in Burundi. Where is Burundi?* followed by, *I think I'm supposed to tell somebody I got this call. What do we do?*

During the summer in DC, a lot of officers take time off, and as a result, interns are exposed to even more opportunities than they may normally be exposed to. That was the situation I found myself in. Over the next week, I began to see the inner workings of different parts of the State Department and who was involved in the work that we did at the UN. I was fortunate to have a boss who brought me into the room to listen in on the series of conference calls and meetings that followed. Junior staffers and interns like me were called upon to do much of the research on the region to get everyone up to speed, and I was excited to draw on all the knowledge I had gathered from my African and African American studies degree.

I had the privilege of sitting in the meetings for and supporting then–US Permanent Representative to the UN Madeleine Albright in drafting the document that would become one of the US resolutions on Burundi. In 1996, Ambassador Albright was one of the few women seated around the table filled predominately by white men, but being the only one did not reduce her impact. Ambassador Albright (later Secretary Albright) was a force who commanded her space at the table. She was also someone who acknowledged the work that was done, and if you were the one providing research information, even if you were just an intern, you were the one to whom she directed her questions, and she expected you to be able to answer. It was intimidating and exhilarating all at once.

As a young foreign service officer (FSO or diplomat in layman's terms) in training at my first internship post, I was very conscious of my position. I considered what I wore and how I entered a room. When I look back at pictures of me from when I was in my twenties in the Foreign Service, it's clear that I went overboard on the professional look and dressed much older than my age. I'm almost fifty, and those clothes look too old for me now! I went to the extreme because I was always worried that if I showed up "wrong," it would reflect on something bigger than me—a reflection on the Black FSOs? A reflection on Ambassador Davis and the Pickering Fellowship program?

This was a period when I was told I needed to wear blacks, browns, and grays and to not stand out with the intent of going unnoticed. I would hear that, but at the same time, I'd think, *But if I'm the only or one of the few Black people in the room, how am I not going to be noticed? If I am the only or one of the few women in the room, how am I not going to be noticed?*

In these State Department meetings, there was always a big conference table with chairs all around it and a secondary row of chairs that were placed along the edges of the wall. Even if I was the first person in the room, I would always gravitate toward that back row, usually sitting in a corner. One morning (while she may not remember, it will forever be ingrained in my mind), Assistant Secretary of State for African Affairs Susan Rice told me, "If you come in the room and there's a seat at the table, you take it. Because when they come in the room, they're going to take it." Years later, I would understand what had been offered to me that day: the knowledge that I, too, a young Black woman, belonged at the table and that I had the power to claim my seat. Susan Rice *chose* to see me, my value, and my potential. (Susan Rice is a Stanford alum too … go Chocolate Cardinal!)

The guidance and counsel so freely offered to me by so many strong, capable, and confident women leaders are not something I take lightly. I believe that it is an honor and my duty to pay attention to every opportunity in which I can offer that same level of guidance and counsel to those coming up behind me.

At the close of my internship, I barely had time to take a breath before I was on my way to begin my studies at Princeton in the fall of 1996.

CHAPTER 6
FIGHT SONG

"Fight Song"

Like a small boat on the ocean sending big waves into motion
Like how a single word can make a heart open
I might only have one match, but I can make an explosion

—Rachel Platten

rinceton provided me with an outstanding education, but for me, personally, it was a truly isolating time. In the second year of my master's program, I was the only Black woman across two cohorts of students, and throughout my time there, most of my professors and faculty were older white men. Their perspectives were very different from mine. After spending four years in the Stanford environment that had been so affirming of my identity and so diverse in its faculty, voices, and perspectives, it was challenging to exist in an environment that was devoid of the diversity of people and perspectives that had made Stanford my game changer.

As a Pickering Fellow, my security clearance needed to be periodically updated. One of those updates occurred during my second year at Princeton. The process is extensive. You provide the security clearance team members with the names of three people to interview for background checks. And then they begin their walk-around. They interview the three people, and then they ask each of them to provide three names of people they know who know you. Those three people are then interviewed and asked to provide the names of three more, and it continues to a level they are satisfied with.

The security clearance team came to Princeton to interview me, asked me for my three references, and then walked around my graduate program office asking various people if they knew me, explaining that the team was doing a background check. As Princeton was a policy school, people understood background checks and weren't surprised by them. I would learn later that there was a group of four white students in my cohort whose responses to the background questions were extreme outliers to all the other interviews. I had been in class with them for a year and a half, and they said, "We don't really know DeAngela or what she does. She's extra private, and no one really knows where she is or what she's doing, so there might be more for you to investigate."

That response was so negative and out of character compared with all the other people the team interviewed that the interviewer asked me if I had gotten in a fight or had an issue with any of my classmates. I was as surprised as she was and told her that I didn't have an issue with anyone. I said that I engaged in the classroom with those students but not outside of the classroom because we just didn't move in the same circles.

That was my personal Princeton experience—that feeling of not being supported and that sense that some chose to believe it was only my fellowship that got me there, much in the same way some people view affirmative action. They chose to believe that I did not earn my spot.

Fortunately, both HOBY and Stanford had so grounded me in my own value, what I brought to the table, and where I wanted to go that even though I felt like the people in my program didn't see me or value who I was and the credentials I brought to the table, I knew I belonged in that elite program. I had just graduated with honors from Stanford with a dual degree. How they chose to see me was their issue, not mine. I committed myself to taking full advantage of that opportunity to get myself where I wanted to go. I knew I just had to put my head down and push through to the other side.

One of my anchors during that time was my high school sweetheart, Kelly. He was one of the people who helped push me through and kept me grounded during that period. He and I had been on and off again since I had gone off to Stanford. When I returned home for visits and summers during that period, it was so easy to let myself fall into the feeling of home that Kelly evoked in me. But just like in high school, when he jumped into the fray, running down the halls and fighting, and I opted to try to dialogue with the powers that be, we continued to interact with life in very different ways. I was highly focused on what I wanted and how I was going to get it, and Kelly was still finding his own path, with a few starts and stalls.

Despite our differences, Kelly remained my place of peace. We had so much shared history, and with Kelly, I wasn't a student or an FSO in training. I didn't have to interact or do things in a certain way. I was just me, Dee from around the block, and that was incredibly comforting to me. I had my own apartment while at Princeton, and Kelly lived with me through much of that time.

There were other people who also helped me push through my time at Princeton. Amazing, beautiful people who would stay with me for the rest of my life.

I think early on in our careers, we think about mentors like the Ambassador Davises who are decades ahead of us because we look for the person we can, at some point in the distant future, aspire to be. And then we find someone like Carmen Twillie Ambar, who is more of a peer but is two or three steps ahead of us in life and career—a person we can be inspired to be in the moment.

Carmen, a smart, accomplished, formidable Black woman, was an administrator at Princeton during my time there. Carmen didn't just mentor me on what steps to take to get here or there; she talked to me about the practical stuff, such as how to move through life as a young professional with dreams and a career and balance all that with family and everything I wanted for my future. Carmen kept it real, sharing with me what had worked and hadn't worked for her and the challenges and frustrations that she had faced. Because she was so close to me in age and our journeys were so similar, in Carmen, I could see all my possibilities.

Toward the end of my tenure at Princeton, Carmen and I worked together to create infrastructure to better recruit and support Black students who entered our highly selective graduate program. Carmen would go on to serve as president of Cedar Crest College and then Oberlin College, blazing a path I believed I just might follow.

Kevin was another pivotal person in my time at Princeton. He was a senior in an undergraduate program when I was a first-year grad student. I remember walking past Kevin, who was standing in front of what I would learn was Princeton's cultural center, and exchanging hellos. He invited me into the cultural center, which was then called the Third World Center. "Seriously," I said, "The cultural center is called the Third World Center," followed by, "and Princeton only has one cultural center?"

Stanford offered such a rich celebration of identity and culture, which is why Princeton felt so stark to me in contrast. But Kevin helped me see that there were culturally rich aspects of Princeton; they were just less visible and less systemic than they were at Stanford. Princeton's Third World Center was the hub for Black undergraduates and other students of color. On Thursday or Friday nights, wafting from the multipurpose room where we all gathered might be the aroma of Caribbean, African, Soul, or Latin cuisine or a combination of varied ethnic cuisines. The food was provided by students, staff, and local ethnic restaurants in the area.

Music was always playing, and just like at so many of my family gatherings at Granny's, people were gathered around small tables, engaged in games of dominoes, spades, or bid whist. You didn't need to know everyone's name (and they didn't need to know yours) to be greeted with, "Hey, how you doing?" followed by an offering of food or a seat at a table.

It was the space that felt most like home to me in an environment that, in many ways, felt so foreign. Kevin and Princeton's Black undergraduate life would sustain me through my first year there and would lead me to my connection with other grad students through the Black Graduate Caucus, which would serve as my support and sustenance during my second and final year at Princeton. Kevin and I would go on to do a tremendous amount of access work together beyond the walls of Princeton.

There are strengths that are developed in moments of challenge, and those challenges at Princeton pushed me to create a circle of support outside of the isolated space my master's program provided me. Dr. Richard Hope would often set me straight when I was feeling particularly challenged. I knew Dr. Hope through my Pickering Fellowship—he was one of its founders—and he was on faculty at Princeton and ran our fellowship through the Woodrow Wilson National Fellowship Foundation. I can remember many times sitting in his office and telling him that I didn't like it there or that I didn't like the people there.

I can still hear him saying, "Now, DeAngela, you're at Princeton. You're at the Woodrow Wilson School of Public and International Affairs. This is the best opportunity. This is your moment. You're not here to make friends. You're not here to love it. You know what you're here for; now go do what you're supposed to do."

Dr. Hope was right. At Princeton, I received one of the most amazing public policy educations. I understand that, and I understood it then, and I'm so appreciative of the opportunity to be part of such a selective process and how important and powerful that was for me. The truth is that I can do what I do from a data and policy standpoint because of the training that I received there.

My education at Princeton has enabled me to level the playing field for those who haven't believed they belonged or haven't been able to access higher education or other environments. It was worth the isolation, and I believe it was necessary for what was to come.

CHAPTER 7
CAN YOU STAND THE RAIN

"Can You Stand the Rain"

Sunny days, everybody loves them
Tell me ... can you stand the rain?

—New Edition

n the summer of 1997, after my first year of graduate school, I was slated to go to Eritrea for my second Pickering FSO internship, which I was so excited about. Eritrea is adjacent to Ethiopia, and there was so much happening in that part of the world. With my BA in international relations and African/African American studies, I was halfway through my MPA in public policy and international affairs, so the internship aligned well with my research, my passions, and my interests.

That spring, just weeks before I was to leave, we lost Granny—everyone's Aunt Peaches. I remember my mom's voice on the other end of the phone telling me that Granny had had a stroke and that she was in bad shape and wouldn't be with us for much longer. I was twenty-two, and Granny was my first significant loss. After that call, I sat in the window seat of my Princeton apartment, staring out across the campus with its array of formidable stone buildings interspersed with clusters of trees and feeling so alone and so desperate to get home to my family. Back then, booking a flight and arranging transportation to and from the airport wasn't as simple as it is today. It would take three days to get me home, arriving one day after Granny was gone.

It was my first memory of feeling like my choices were often selfish. If I hadn't selfishly decided to go to school so far from home, I would have made it back in time to say goodbye to Granny. I kept playing over in my head how I was the only grandkid who chose to move so far away, and I was always the one missing important family moments. I felt consumed with this illogical feeling of acting selfishly because I had chosen not to remain in Kansas City. This feeling would inform my decision to request a change to my international Foreign Service internship, from Eritrea to somewhere within a four-hour flight. I simply couldn't bear to think of being so far from home.

My dad's family is big. Jason and I have so many aunts, uncles, and cousins, and we all returned to Granny's home after her funeral. How we gathered at Granny's that day was the same way we always gathered at Granny's. On every available surface sat pies, a turkey ready to be carved, and any number of other comfort foods we so often shared. In the absence of food, the surfaces were covered in dominoes or playing cards. There was laughing, talking, and sharing of stories. Granny had raised us all that way. It was a day for family and celebration, not sorrow.

It wouldn't take long for all of us grandkids (most of us adults or nearly adults at the time) to settle together on the long stairway leading up to the second floor. It was not uncommon for groups of us cousins to sit there over the years, mostly to find our own private space away from the eyes and ears of the adults, to talk, play, or gossip. On that day, we were quiet as we sat on those stairs, contemplating how we would navigate a world without Granny. The one thing I knew for certain in that moment was that I was going to stay as close to home as the Foreign Service would allow.

My request to remain within a four-hour flight to Kansas City was not welcomed, and it narrowed my options to North or Central America. I didn't know Spanish, but I did know French, and so, after some negotiating with the help of Dr. Hope, I was sent to Canada. Although it had been my decision to change, it was still disappointing to think that of all the places I could go, I would be spending my summer internship somewhere as unexciting as Ottawa, Canada.

But, just like my choosing the Pickering Fellowship over my dream of the Coca-Cola Olympics Fellowship, my Canadian internship turned out to be better than I could have ever imagined.

As a Pickering fellow, I had full-level top secret clearance—access that most interns only dream of. Pickering taught us State Department processes, lingo, and systems. By the time I was heading to Canada, I already had my domestic internship under my belt, and I knew how to write memos and briefings. Pickering had prepared me well, and I was ready.

That summer of 1997, Canada was preparing to host the Asia-Pacific Economic Cooperation (APEC) Summit in November. The US and Canada were members of APEC. In the lead-up to the summit, each president's ministerial sectors came together to work through their policies, which would then be put forward by their presidents in the fall. I had the privilege to not only sit in all the US ministerial policy meetings but to also take notes and write up synopses, which I then sent via cable back to Washington. Translated into US terms, *ministerials* included cabinet-level secretaries from all over the world. It was an amazing learning opportunity for me to have a front-row seat to critical policy discussions among the secretary of commerce, the secretary of transportation, US trade representatives, and others.

Canada wasn't Eritrea, but I was OK with that because it was a phenomenal experience that provided me with mentors who exuded Black excellence and whom I could see myself in. Their impact would stay with me and guide me as I moved through my career in the Foreign Service and beyond.

At the time, the senior trade policy advisor in the Office of International Transportation and Trade was Florie Liser. To observe how the secretary of transportation commanded a room was amazing, but to see how he leaned on Florie for her expertise and to see Florie move in and out of that space while commanding her expertise and helping her principal move and navigate provided me with real-time lessons that I would carry with me throughout my career. The secretary of transportation and Senior Trade Policy Advisor Liser gave a master class on how to staff a principal, how to be a principal, and how to show up in that space as a principal and as a person of color without apologies or excuses.

Because transportation was such a key part of economic trade, I crossed Florie's path multiple times that summer. Florie always showed up as a strong Black woman, wearing braids long before African Americans were walking around with our authentic hair, and she made sure that I understood how to be seen in the spaces I was moving in. I remember one time, as we were walking into the ministerial meetings, someone asked me to go get coffee. As I turned to do that, Florie grabbed my arm and said, "I understand you are an intern, but you are serving as their control officer for this visit. Control officers do not go get coffee. You either show them where the coffee is or send someone to get their coffee."

I left Ottawa at the end of the summer and returned to my graduate studies at Princeton. In October, I received a call from Sigrid Emrich, economics section chief. Sigrid had been my boss and an amazing source of support during my internship. That night, she said, "The APEC leaders' meeting is in November in Vancouver, and we are putting together the team that will be supporting US Trade Representative Barshefsky."

"Yes," I said, "how can I be helpful? Do you need my notes from this summer?"

Sigrid's deep and joyful laugh filled my ear, "No, Dee, we need you to come back and serve as Barshefsky's deputy control officer. You prepped every ministerial last summer. We know you're up to speed on all of this and are exactly what we need."

My response was, "When do you want me there?" And off I went, back to Canada—Vancouver this time, where I lived in a hotel room for about three weeks in the middle of the fall semester of my second year of grad school. (It was my friend and mentor, Carmen Ambar, who helped me negotiate the time away from school, telling me to remind my professors that Princeton was a policy school, and this was a prime opportunity for me to develop my policy-making skills.) In those magical three weeks, I had the privilege of sitting in spaces and places with the presidents of the APEC nations. I met President Clinton and his staff. During my time in the ministerial meetings and serving as Barshefsky's deputy control officer during the summit, I soaked in every piece of knowledge I was exposed to. I listened, I learned, and I made connections with people who would become lifelong colleagues for me.

There were many important lessons I learned during my Canadian internship, but one of the most vital ones was this: Even if you are "just" the person taking notes, when you consistently show up and deliver quality work, good leaders pay attention. While I was incredibly fortunate to be called back to serve as deputy control officer, it wasn't by happenstance that I got that call. All summer, I had shown up and delivered quality work, and my amazing supervisor, Sigrid Emrich, had noticed. She was paying attention, so when the time came to fill the role of deputy control officer for Barshefsky, she willingly opened yet another door for me. She knew I could deliver, not like a grad student or an intern, but like the FSO the fellowship had trained me to be.

CHAPTER 8

I'M GONNA BE READY

"I'm Gonna Be Ready"

You know what's best for me
Prepare my mind, prepare my heart
For whatever comes, I'm gon' be ready

—Yolanda Adams

One night in the summer of 1999, as I sat on my sofa listening to my Mandarin language tapes, my phone rang. I answered it and heard my name spoken in a very distinct voice. I jumped from my sofa and stood at attention, "Ambassador Davis," I said with slight alarm. "How can I help you?"

By this time, I had completed my master's program at Princeton and had entered the Foreign Service. I was just finishing up a year-long training period in DC at the FSI in preparation for my first post as an FSO. I was to be stationed in Beijing. My new adventure, which I had been preparing for since the spring of 1994, when I received the Pickering Fellowship, had finally arrived.

"A conversation is going to come to you tomorrow," Ambassador Davis said. "Your career officer is going to inform you that there is a need in a country that they believe you can fill. They need you to take this stretch position because you have the language and the general services officer training, and they need someone at post immediately. It is an eight-month gap that you will be filling. It will require you to switch your rotation from Beijing to Guangzhou, China."

I began to sputter, "I can do this. That's fine, Ambassador Davis. I think I can adjust ..."

"DeAngela," the ambassador said, interrupting my sputtering. I stood a bit taller. "I am calling you for you to understand that when the Foreign Service calls you as a commissioned officer, as a generalist, it is your responsibility to meet that need and to serve. But with every turn and with every request, you need to be prepared for what you need and want for yourself and for your career, particularly as a young, Black female officer. The reason I am calling you," she continued, "is that I want you to be prepared to tell them what you want in exchange."

That was a game-changing moment for me. Ambassador Davis gave me a voice in which direction I wanted to go. While she made it abundantly clear that I would be accepting the Guangzhou post, Ambassador Davis also made clear that it was my abilities and credentials that provided me this stretch opportunity. Even though I was a brand-new FSO, I had already completed two tours with the State Department through my Pickering Fellowship internships. I had been a control officer for a cabinet-level presidential visit in Canada, and I had served on the UN desk at a critical time during the coup in Burundi and more. I also had the necessary management and language training needed. Ambassador Davis and all the other mentors I engaged with through my Pickering Fellowship had prepared me for this moment—a moment in which I would begin to learn how to navigate the spaces and places that were historically closed off to someone like me.

With that call, Ambassador Davis helped me sort out the positives and negatives of this post change. The Guangzhou post would provide me with the opportunity to experience the whole portfolio of the management officer rather than just one aspect of that work, which was what I would be limited to in Beijing. But Guangzhou processed different visas from Beijing. The government was very focused on processing visas for families who were adopting children from China. In Beijing, I would be exposed to all the different types of visa work and support American citizen services. And I really wanted the big city experience. I wanted the Disney World of China, and the small province of Guangzhou was far from that. I told Ambassador Davis that the biggest piece was losing the opportunity to do my visa work in Beijing. "They need you in Guangzhou to fill a gap for a period. After that period, they will make an opening for you in their visa rotation. Beijing has such a demand for visas that they will always have openings there, so you tell them what you want."

And that's exactly what I did.

At the end of that training year in DC, there was another call. But this was a call initiated by me. When I left Princeton and headed to DC, Kelly returned to Kansas City. We saw very little of each other during that year, and when we did, I realized that our differences were creating tensions that could no longer be avoided. Here I was at twenty-five, headed overseas to begin my Foreign Service career, while Kelly, at twenty-four, had yet to find his path. I just didn't see how we could make it work, so I called and told him it was over, and in

September of 1999, I made my way to Guangzhou to begin my first official post as an FSO.

My dad decided he would fly to China with me to make sure I arrived OK. If my Granny had still been with us, I truly believe she would have told my dad, "Jerome, you better go with that baby and check this place out." Our first stop was Beijing so that I could be briefed, and then together, we flew on to Guangzhou. My dad's visit was quick—about forty-eight hours. His air travel time almost exceeded his time on the ground. But it was long enough for me to share a bit of the unknown in my work.

In Beijing, we stayed overnight at the InterContinental hotel before we headed down to Guangzhou. My dad hung out in the hotel room most of our arrival day, as I was immediately immersed in the briefing process. On my way back to our room at the end of the day, I found my dad sitting in the lobby. I asked him what he was doing there and whether everything was OK with the room.

"Well," he said, "they just kept coming in and coming in and then leaving when they saw me there. Finally, I just went downstairs so they could clean the room."

I knew why they "kept coming in," and it wasn't to clean our room. I wanted to explain to my dad without alarming him. "Daddy," I explained, "the reason they kept coming in to see if the room was empty wasn't because they wanted to clean the room. It was so they could search the room."

He thought about it and said, "Yeah, there was a point when I thought I saw a quick camera flicker."

I told him that it was possible and explained that having our room and belongings searched was a part of diplomatic life in a Communist country.

"But they didn't take nothing?" he asked.

"No, they don't take anything. It's obvious that we're foreigners, and they just wanted to see what we brought."

What struck me in that moment was how different the space I was navigating then was from my life and my family's life in Kansas City. I understood something my dad was just learning about, and while I wanted to share it with him, I also wanted to protect him from unnecessary worries. Having just traveled to Beijing, he realized it would take him at least a full day in air travel time alone to get back to me if I needed him, and I wanted to be sensitive to that.

When it was time to get him to the airport for his return home, I thought I could figure out how to get him there. I knew the language, and I knew how to navigate new places. But Guangzhou was not just any place, and it wasn't long before I grew frantic about how I could get my dad to the airport safely and on time.

I finally asked my assistant for help. "I need to figure out how to get my dad to the airport. Who do I talk to? Who can help me?"

She began to giggle, and I thought, *What am I missing, and why is she laughing at me?* Still smiling, she said, "You control everything at the consulate. The motor pool and the people to get your father through immigration and customs report to you. You just tell us what to do." And so began my Foreign Service career.

I had never had trouble taking the lead, but the responsibility of overseeing the operational aspects of a US consulate in China with a staff of thirty-five Chinese nationals was a lot for a young twenty-something. And that I, as a junior officer in this stretch position, was now serving in a role more senior than my current rank was intimidating. In my time there, I came to understand that the decisions I made impacted the lives of those around me, which in turn, could impact the lives of those around them. This was something I would learn to respect, appreciate, and honor in how I lead.

CHAPTER 9
LIFT ME UP

"Lift Me Up"

Lift me up. Hold me down
Keep me safe. Keep me close.
Safe and sound

—Rihanna

It's just a screwdriver, I thought as I reread the evidence against a member of the US consulate staff. *Do I really need to fire him over this*?"

I had been at my post in Guangzhou for about four months and had just received confirmation that one of the consulate staff members I supervised had, over time, stolen a set of tools—the latest of which was a screwdriver. Like me, he, too, was a young twenty-something, and I couldn't help but wonder if the recommendation for termination was the right option.

There was a second question that also gnawed at me: *Am I capable of firing someone?* I didn't know.

Because the Guangzhou consulate was so small and because of the way we moved and communicated with each other, we weren't as formal as I would learn other consulates were. There were maybe eighty of us in total: a combination of American FSOs and specialists and Chinese nationals all working in the same building. The first three floors were office spaces, and the top three-plus floors housed the FSOs. We each had our own apartment. The apartment of the consul general, the most senior-ranking officer at the mission, was designed to provide both living and functional spaces, including an office, a conference room, and a dining/living area to entertain dignitaries. It was not uncommon for me and other junior officers to be included in meetings there, along with the consul general's senior team. Without fuss or proclivity to ranking, we would all scoot our chairs around the large mahogany wood table and discuss what was occurring in the country, what needed to be monitored, and who was responsible for which actions.

There was a genuine familiarity with which we all functioned. Working (and for some of us, living) so closely together, we were, in many ways, like a family. We picked up lunch or cups of coffee for each other. The Foreign Service personnel hosted social events at the consulate for both the personnel and their family members who were in the country and the staff of Chinese nationals and their families. Having immersed myself in this work family, I was now expected to fire one of its members? How would that impact the team? And I also wondered how it would look for a young Black woman, new to the consulate and her role in it, to start firing people.

I knew this was the job I signed up for, but I also knew that, in this instance, I needed guidance on how to make the right decision. I locked myself in my office and sat at my desk, and as I reached for the phone,

I felt as if I were teetering at the top of a roller coaster, grasping for the brake. This was not an easy phone call to make. As a junior FSO, you want to appear ready, confident, and knowledgeable when you arrive at post. I didn't yet understand the parameters of what I could share or how much my original mentor assigned to me when I entered the Pickering Fellowship would understand my hesitation to take action.

My mentor did understand, and her response was direct. "There are standards you must abide by. People will respect you for what you do and how you handle it, but be sure to do it with dignity—there's no need to embarrass the staff person." I knew she was right.

As part of our training in the Foreign Service, it is made very clear that we must be above reproach as much as possible. No matter how small the infraction, it opens the door for others to use that infraction against you to gain favor or to coerce you into committing other infractions. One small, unchecked infraction could also embolden an individual to commit further infractions—as was the case with this young man. The infraction itself, no matter how insignificant, isn't the issue. It's the circumstance; it's the environment; it's the sensitivity of working in a consulate in a Communist country. It's your credibility and your reputation as an officer in the Foreign Service. In this work, your reputation is currency.

Still, I allowed myself to continue teetering—to not yet make the decision. I had great respect for my senior staff members, both of whom were Chinese nationals, and I sought out their advice too. Without hesitation, they told me, "He must go. He cannot stay. If you think he steals, you think we all steal." The earnestness with which they shared their opinions helped me understand the culture I was working and leading within and, most critically, the level of accountability to which they held each other—family or not. The impact of how I handled this situation was bigger than just this one individual. But that individual still mattered to me.

The image that sticks most vividly in my mind about this experience is how imposing my dark, heavy wooden desk felt as I sat on one side and the young man sat on the other. I fought to keep my hands still and my voice steady, and the young man, head bowed, looked only at his hands, folded and still in his lap. Because termination is a matter of HR, there was no room for potential language barriers, necessitating my assistant, Jamie, to sit beside him and translate from my English to his Cantonese and from his Cantonese to my English. The latter translation was minimal. The young man never looked up, and the only words he spoke were, "I did it. I'm sorry. I understand." There was no protest, only submission.

I knew that, for him and his family, the weight of losing a position at the US consulate was enormous. Even though he did not serve in a high-level position, simply having a job at the consulate was prestigious. It provided his family with better housing, access to vehicles, and an elevated income level. With his termination, all of that could disappear.

When they left my office, I closed the door behind them and once again sat down at my desk. This time, instead of reaching for the phone to call my mentor, I put my head in my hands and let my tears flow. I had never fired anyone before, and I didn't want to ever do it again.

This was the first time I understood that there was power in my power. Not in terms of wielding power over people but how my own power could impact others. More importantly, I began to understand my responsibility in exercising that power with *care*. The foundation of faith that my family instilled in me—kindness, compassion, and a belief that everyone has value—held true in all instances and was something I had to anchor myself in as I navigated my current role as an FSO and in all my leadership roles to come.

Between Guangzhou and Beijing, I spent more than two years in China, and I immersed myself in the experience. When you love cultures and languages like I do, the greatest gift you can receive when visiting, working, or living in another country is not to be seen as an outsider or a tourist. The less you seem like an outsider, the more likely the citizens of the country will introduce you to places and people that they would introduce a friend to. In China, although it was challenging to look at me and not see an outsider, it was important to me to be accepted by the Chinese people. Because I spoke the language and I was genuinely interested in the people and their culture, I was accepted in many circles and conversations.

Through these experiences, I came to learn that in the Chinese culture, the history of where your people come from is passed down from generation to generation. No matter where people of Chinese descent are born in the world, their lineage is sacred. When I explored outside of the embassy in Beijing, many people assumed I was a student studying in China. They also assumed that I was African and that I had come to China from Africa. When I clarified that I was African American and that I had arrived from America, there would be confusion. "Yes," they would say, "but you're African. Where are your people from?" In those moments, I was forced to acknowledge that I did not know where my people came from.

The idea that someone could not know where their family came from was incomprehensible to them. "You don't know where your family descends from?" they would ask, astonished. "Why, what happened?" I found myself struggling to find the words that could explain the Middle Passage—the time period between the 1500s to the 1800s when merchants captured and forced approximately twelve million Africans onto ships and transported them across the Atlantic to be sold into slavery in Europe and the Americas.

I remember getting on the phone and calling my language instructor at the FSI—a short, round Chinese man who made my life hell for seven months so that I could be fluent in Mandarin. "Nǐ xiǎng yào shénm? (What do you want?)" he asked gruffly. I explained to him that I found China beautiful, I loved it, and it was exciting to be connecting with everyday people outside of the embassy. And then I told him about my recent conversation with a taxi driver about where my people were from and how I felt at a loss as to how to explain the Middle Passage to them. When I finished, he made me say it all again but in Chinese. After I ended with "Middle Passage" the second time around, he grumbled and told me that my tones were off, and then he had me explain the Middle Passage to him in English.

He provided me with the words to explain why I didn't know where my people came from. We are descendants of African kings and queens who ruled the continent of Africa, I would explain in Mandarin. And we are American because my ancestors were taken from the shores of Africa, put on boats, and brought to America to be enslaved. America is all my family and I have ever known. We were born there; that is our home. My journey is American. I'm a proud African American. My journey, my story, and my face are America.

It felt amazing for me to be able to share that story in Mandarin. Often, the response would be, "Oh, your people are strong. They survived. They are strong like us."

The telling of my story and my journey, helping people see all the things that make up who I am to find that common ground when they see themselves in my story and I see myself in theirs, was a profound experience for me. That, to me, was my China journey, in so many ways.

When I completed my posts in China, I finally made my way to Africa—not to Eritrea but to a post in Pretoria, South Africa, in September of 2001. There, I found an amazing group of women who needed no explanation of the Middle Passage or what it meant to be an African American.

Uniting Many on Our Journey Through Africa (UMOJA) is a women's organization created by a group of African American women who were US officers or spouses of officers from many different agencies, such as the State Department, the Peace Corps, and the United States Agency for International Development, living and working in South Africa. UMOJA was a way for them to stay connected and to keep their children connected to our culture, which is incredibly difficult when living overseas for many years.

I was a welcome member of the group of UMOJA families in Pretoria. We met every month, and we ran activities for the kids, such as a Black History Month program and a Martin Luther King program. We had picnics at each other's houses and played cards. We celebrated birthdays together. We all went to church together at a small, primarily Black church that one of the women of UMOJA had started with her husband. I did not go to church in China, and I had missed it.

Being welcomed into their church in Pretoria felt like coming home. I was fortunate to have had that same feeling of walking into Paradise Missionary Church—a feeling of coming home to a church, first as a student at Stanford, not on the college campus but in a small Black church in East Palo Alto. It was a drive from the campus, and I did not own a car, but I did find other students who were also drawn to this church, and the group of us would carpool. And then again, years later, when I returned to Stanford as a member of its administration, I was invited by a woman who became a dear friend, Shirley Everett, to her church in Livermore, St. Matthew's Baptist Church. This was another small Black church community that made me feel like I had walked back in time and into Paradise. UMOJA offered me that same sense of community and home in so many ways.

UMOJA was a social network that enabled us to provide ourselves and each other with support during our time away from home and opportunities to just exhale for a moment and enjoy ourselves. But this influential, powerful community of Black American servicewomen also embodied a tremendous sense of gratitude and service toward the country that was our host.

South Africa had opened its doors for our families to do this work, and we felt an immense need to show our appreciation and to give back. Every year, we identified a local charity and held a fundraiser to support their work. These fundraisers did more than raise money; they drew us closer into the community in which we were living and allowed us to better know and understand the citizens of our host country. UMOJA's mindset of giving back is, unfortunately, not all that common among the foreign diplomats who are citizens of first-world countries. When they serve in third-world countries, they often display an attitude of superiority and a mindset that they are there to "fix" or "save" the citizens of their host country.

I am so proud to still be a part of such an amazing group of women who serve the world with gratitude and integrity. They have helped me thrive, learn, grow, and sometimes simply survive. I spent two years at my post in South Africa, and these women were always there when I needed them. They continue to be one of my circles of support today. We recently brought together more than thirty families for a UMOJA reunion in DC. Many of us had not seen each other in more than twenty years, but beautifully, it was like we never left South Africa or each other.

While my immersion in UMOJA was an incredibly smooth transition, the months leading up to my scheduled September 13, 2001, departure and my actual arrival in South Africa were anything but.

CHAPTER 10
JUST FINE

"Just Fine"

Got my head on straight, I got my vibe right
You see I wouldn't change my life,
My life's just ... Fine, fine, fine, fine, fine, fine, ooooh

—Mary J. Bligé

Over the holiday season leading into 2001, ten months before my scheduled departure to Africa, I spent my twenty-eight-day leave from Beijing in Kansas City with my family. Kelly and I had been broken up for almost two years by then, but we stayed connected through letters and phone calls here and there. When he heard I was home and asked if I wanted to hang out, I was happy to let myself temporarily fall back into the comfort of our old relationship. As New Year's Eve approached, Kelly and I made plans to go to his cousin's New Year's party together, just as we had done every year since we began dating in high school. My leave, our time together, and our plans for New Year's Eve were all so familiar and uneventful … until they weren't.

We had left his cousin's place shortly after midnight with plans to hang out with friends at the hotel where we were staying. I can remember just kind of winding down, and I was talking to our friends on the phone. As I hung up the call, I turned around and nearly fell over Kelly, who was down on one knee, looking up at me with a ring in his hand.

I was stunned into silence, but only for a moment before I blurted out, "What are you doing?" followed by, "Get up, get up, don't do this."

But Kelly was committed, and there he stayed, planted on one knee. "I want to spend my life with you. You can't go back to China without putting this ring on your finger."

"Get up, get up," I said again. "When I leave China, I'm not coming home. I'm going to South Africa."

"I'll go wherever you go," he said.

He wouldn't stop talking, and I wouldn't give an answer because all I could think was that this didn't make sense. We weren't even together. Eventually, the answer I gave was, "You need to talk to my parents." He did, and my parents had their reservations as I knew they (and many others) would, but they also supported whatever I chose.

Two days later, I would put the ring on. The memory I have of that moment is of Kelly sitting in the chair by the window in my childhood bedroom and me sitting on the bed. In the corner between the two of us was a beautiful globe that I had shipped home from China. After I finally said yes, Kelly started spinning the globe in search of South Africa. When his finger landed on it, he said, "So this is where we're going." And then with a smile, he added, "I've always wanted to go to Africa." I can tell you in those heartbeats of time, I felt immense comfort knowing that, for the first time along this journey that took me so far from home, I would have a partner to share this amazing experience with me. A partner who felt like home to me, a partner who really knew me, a partner I could fully be myself with. Kelly was all those things. And our time together in South Africa would turn out to be truly magical.

At the end of my leave that holiday season, I returned to my post in Beijing, and with my mom's support and event planning expertise, she and I planned my wedding from different continents over the next several months. Kelly and I were married in Granny's church, my home church, Paradise Missionary Baptist, on August 8, 2001. Our wedding day was even more beautiful than I had dreamed it would be, and I can dream big. I am a Mickey Mouse fanatic, and if we couldn't get married in Disney, I was determined to bring Disney to Paradise. We had a Mickey and Minnie wedding cake topper, mouse-eared cupcakes, and Disney champagne flutes. Kelly's best friend, Jamal, even wore a Mickey costume during most of our reception. He was the real hero that day. Kelly and I would spend our honeymoon immersed in Disney World, wearing our Disney bride and groom T-shirts and having our picture taken with Mickey and Minnie every chance we could (really every chance *I* could—Kelly wasn't a Mickey fan). It was truly a magical week that was over all too quickly. We returned home to pack and prepare for our first stop in DC to process all the paperwork for my next post and then fly on to South Africa, but our flights to South Africa on September 13, 2001, would never happen.

Two days earlier, on September 11, 2001, terrorists hijacked planes departing from Boston, DC, and Newark and crashed them into the twin towers in New York City and the Pentagon in DC. All travel in and out of the US was immediately halted on September 11, and it would be another three weeks before Kelly and I were on one of the first flights out of the DC area and making our way to Pretoria. I would eventually come to see firsthand the impact of those terrorist attacks on the work we were doing around the world.

For most Americans, 9/11 would change their world. It would change my world, including my job and eventually my entire career trajectory. Being in DC that day, we felt the impact when the plane hit the Pentagon, physically and psychologically. I was scheduled to visit the Pentagon the next day as part of my out-briefing process. For those of us in the Foreign Service, 9/11 and its aftermath weren't something we watched on TV; it was intertwined in our work—in my life's work.

Since the early days of my Pickering Fellowship, I had dreamed of serving in Africa. That dream was now my reality—a reality overshadowed by the current state of the world—but the work had to continue regardless. I was in public affairs, and our work focused on public outreach, stakeholder engagement, media, education, and more. One of our major initiatives at the time was working with nonprofits in the communities that were building infrastructure and resources to fight the AIDS epidemic that had engulfed the country. We were providing dollars through our programs and other US federal government programs to build health clinics—and not just the physical structures of the clinics but the research connections. Those dollars and our work brought in doctors, specialists, scientists, and trainers.

Our focus was on finding stories about the good work that was happening on the ground across the US mission and all the work happening in South Africa. We found those stories by sitting down with mothers and children in the clinics and asking them about how the clinics were helping them and supporting and changing their communities. We would then ensure that information got to the right places and spaces to amplify the work, and that included coordinating with supporters who brought attention to the cause.

I had the honor of helping to direct the press experience when Nelson Mandela and Jimmy Carter sat down to discuss the epidemic. And I had the privilege of being the lead officer on Bono and Chris Tucker's trip when they came through South Africa to look at the condition of AIDS, antiretrovirals, and AIDS support. It was the work of our team to coordinate these opportunities to shine a light on these very real issues impacting South Africa.

I immersed myself in the work, and I could see the difference we were making.

My service in South Africa exposed me to meaningful work that I loved and incredible leaders who left indelible marks that I would draw upon throughout my career. At my post in South Africa, my senior press attaché, Judy Moon, was one of those incredible leaders.

Judy is a no-nonsense, rambunctious, cargo-pants-wearing woman, who was masterful at what she did. When I joined her post in South Africa, I hadn't been tenured yet. Several months after my arrival, one of the largest situations that our office had ever dealt with came in, and I happened to be the one who picked up the call. The press wanted information. We started to do the research, and we realized that this was going to be a high-profile case. It involved an American citizen who had committed crimes in the US and multiple countries in Africa, and the US government was trying to extradite this person to the United States.

This was a big enough story that *The New York Times* was starting to sniff around and wanted to be able to quote the information that came out of our office. Judy's rule was that the person who picked up a call ran with it from start to finish. They'd get support, but they'd be the lead all the way through. While we were preparing everything, I knew that when it hit, Judy was going to take it—we don't get *The New York Times* in every day from Pretoria.

As we prepared to talk to the press, Judy said to me, "Let me know if you need anything. We can do a prep session if you want."

"What? Me? Aren't you going to take this?" I asked.

Judy was a mid-career officer. For a press officer, getting into *The New York Times* when you were out at a mission and not in DC was huge and could help lead to promotions. I wasn't even a press officer, let alone a mid-career officer, but Judy never hesitated in letting me run with it. Judy had no ego. She wanted the work done, and she wanted to see us all learn and grow.

That level of humility is not always found in the Foreign Service. People are always jockeying for a promotion. In most cases, the work of a junior officer is credited to the senior officer because they directed you to do the work. Judy supported, encouraged, and coached me, but never did she take over or stick her name on it with Washington, the embassy, or the press. She let me be the one quoted in *The New York Times*! To experience Judy's genuine investment in me and excitement for me with such humility still impacts how I lead today. Judy taught me how to be humble enough to say, "I'm already here. I already have the title. I need you to do it. I want to grow you. I want to help you shine."

Being seen for the work that I did and the potential that I had gave me that push to realize that while I might be the youngest or the only woman or the only Black person in the room, I can be recognized for the work that I do. For me, that became a powerful tool because I could then see that I needed to build a reputation for my work. Today, I sit at a point in my career in which my reputation and my work precede me into a room. I no longer worry about being the only or the first or the whatever—even though I still often am—and I no longer dress so that I blend into the background. But it has been an evolution. An evolution that has been fueled by people seeing me and helping me feel like I didn't always have to shoulder the weight of representation alone.

During that time, Kelly and I were also busy building our life together, and the UMOJA community was a huge part of that life. UMOJA provided us with a preexisting community of Black men and women and their families to walk into. In much the same way they supported and guided me, they would do the same for Kelly. Their love and support helped him find his own footing. He enrolled in a sports management program and began coaching a women's basketball team. It was during our time in South Africa that Kelly and I were our very best together. Our second year there, my parents would spend Thanksgiving with us, and then we would all return home together for Christmas. During my parents' visit, I took them to Cape Town, where we visited Table Mountain and Robben Island. To this day, my dad still talks about the emotional experience of standing in the cell where Mandela had stood for eighteen years.

Several of our family members and friends would visit us over that two-and-a-half-year period. My travels with the Foreign Service and the opportunity to share those experiences with my family and friends were a gift I highly valued. To be able to connect my family back home with my newfound UMOJA family in South Africa brought everything full circle for me in such a meaningful way.

Life was so good until a moment in time that changed the trajectory of my life once again.

CHAPTER 11
A CHANGE IS GONNA COME

"A Change Is Gonna Come"

A change gon' come
Oh yes, it will

—Sam Cooke

On March 20, 2003, the US invaded Iraq. I remember receiving the news of the invasion, as the deputy spokesperson for the US embassy in Pretoria, and the talking points that we were directed to deliver to the media. All I could think was, *What in the world are we doing?* This was the beginning of the shift in our work related to the 9/11 attacks. Nelson Mandela immediately came out against the war, and overnight, we became warmongers in the eyes of the South African people. No longer were we thought of as their congenial partner; we had become public enemy number one. Our civilian cars were attacked, US Foreign

Service members picking up their children from school were targeted, and Molotov cocktails were hurled at the embassy.

We were rebriefed on how to use the safe room in our homes. In the two-plus years I had spent in Communist China, not once did I need to consider using the safe room in my home. But now, here in South Africa, I was locking and unlocking security panels. Once we invaded Iraq, our entire foreign policy shifted to winning the war on terrorism, and all the community work we were doing on the ground was stalled. For the first time, I began to wonder about my future with the Foreign Service.

When my tour in South Africa was over in August of 2003, Kelly and I moved back to the States, where I spent what would turn out to be my last year of active duty in the Foreign Service. My new post was as a special assistant for legislative affairs in the Washington, DC, front office in the Bureau of Legislative Affairs. The Bureau of Legislative Affairs coordinates all legislative activity for the Department of State, serves as the department's primary liaison to Congress, and advises the secretary, deputies, undersecretaries, and assistant secretaries on legislative strategy.

My assignment landed me on the seventh floor—the top floor. In this building, all the work flows up. That means all memos, briefings, and requests of other departments or divisions in the State Department come to those of us on the seventh floor who manage everything that goes to the secretariat for that final decision. Being a special assistant in legislative affairs meant that I had direct access to the secretary's office because we were the main entity that controlled what went to Capitol Hill. To land on the seventh floor and to be in that proximity was a big deal. That landing meant you were on the rise in the Foreign Service.

Kelly and I had now been married for two years, and it was time to adapt to married life in the States without the support of our UMOJA community. Jason, my younger brother, had graduated from MU by this time and was living and working in Columbia, Missouri, and looking for new opportunities. I invited him to come and live in DC with us.

Shortly after Jason joined us and settled in, I was in a significant car accident. I was traveling on the Dulles Toll Road in Northern Virginia when my brakes failed. I lost control, careened through the toll gate, hit a tree, and rolled my car. Fortunately, other drivers immediately pulled over, rushed to my aid, and were able to pull me out through the sunroof. Thankfully, I had no broken bones or major external injuries. But because I had been banged around hard when the car rolled, I had deep tissue damage in my hip and leg that required a few months of physical therapy.

I returned home to our apartment with limited mobility and no bladder control. Kelly and Jason took great care of me, keeping me company, making sure I had what I needed, and carting me around to wherever I needed to go for three months. It was another month before I was physically able to get back behind the wheel and then two additional months before I was emotionally ready. My first few months back, I only drove very short distances because I felt like cars were coming at me and things were too close. Kelly and Jason were patient and encouraging, and eventually, I found my confidence.

Those several months in DC together served as a season for the three of us to exist in our own little world and start figuring things out. Kelly worked at the local parks and recreation department during the day and as a security guard at night while Jason worked in IT consulting with Accenture. In the evenings, we would hang out together, watch our favorite TV shows, and frequently test my little brother's stomach of steel. The three of us would make the spiciest foods—foods that Kelly and I thought would definitely be over-the-top even for Jason—but it never failed that long after Kelly and I cried uncle, Jason was powering through, unfazed.

I remember our first tropical storm together (those don't happen in Missouri). We lost power and were at a loss as to how we would keep the food cold. Of course, we called my mom and asked her what we should do. "Just don't open the freezer door too much, or you'll let all the cold out," she advised. "Got it," we told her and then moved on to figuring out how we were going to cook. Luckily, we had a propane grill, so it didn't take us long to solve that problem.

While our time together in DC would create a special bond between the three of us, if I'm honest in my reflections, it was also a time when Kelly and I began to have challenges within our marriage. Several months outside of the fairy-tale world that had been our time in South Africa, the old cracks in our relationship began to reemerge. I was struggling to figure out how to be married *and* how to strengthen my marriage. To go through this struggle in such proximity to my brother was, at times, a point of embarrassment for me. I was his big sister, I was thirty years old, and I felt I should have had my act together on all fronts. By the end of 2003, even the grounding my work had always provided me had begun to feel unstable.

It was in February of 2003 when Secretary Colin Powell made the US case for the invasion of Iraq—a case based on intelligence that showed Saddam Hussein was amassing weapons of mass destruction. That intelligence led the US to invade Iraq in March 2003. By July, the US was fully engulfed in war with Iraq, but no weapons of mass destruction had been uncovered. How our Foreign Service work shifted during this period was very distinct, and by the end of 2003, the concerns being voiced regarding that shift were growing louder.

I remember sitting in a briefing about the Global War on Terror (GWOT) with the members of the Congressional Black Caucus, and the discussion included agreement that while the GWOT was critically important, the members believed there continued to be other critically important issues also going on in the world.

Questions like *Do we not care about what's happening in Haiti? Do we not care about the refugee and migration issues that are growing in Africa? Are we now only concerned about the war?* began to be asked. These discussions were not only happening within the Congressional Black Caucus; debates on how we were showing up in the rest of the world were taking place in every corner of DC. Diplomatic efforts and commitments around the world cannot suddenly be halted and then picked up ten or even six months later. Any pause impacts the countries we have committed to, relationships we have cultivated, and all the foundational work we have done to get us to that point.

FSOs who did not agree with the GWOT began to resign. This is common when major international or political situations occur, creating a sense of misalignment for some of the officers. As for me, I began to ask myself if this new direction our work was going was the work I wanted to be doing and whether this work was positively impacting the communities and lives that I felt committed to. In that last year with the State Department, the answer to those questions was repeatedly no.

I knew I would not remain in the Foreign Service, and over the next few months, I would find clarity in what I wanted to do next.

CHAPTER 12
WHAT IS MY WHY

"What Is My Why"

What's that thing you dream about almost every night?
What gives you drive? What inspires? What lights your fire?
What's the purpose of your life?

—Fearless Motivation

espite my growing concerns over our stalled work within communities around the world, I did find work that brought me joy—work that ultimately led me back to my home away from home, Stanford.

During my post in DC, Secretary Powell developed two key programs that I would be involved in and that would give me the purpose I felt was missing in my everyday work on the seventh floor. One program was called Hometown Diplomats, which served as a marketing and communication campaign to garner goodwill during this time of war and, more importantly, for FSO recruitment purposes.

I was a Hometown Diplomat with a circuit in the Midwest. As such, I would do press engagements and local visits throughout the region to promote the Foreign Service. This was incredibly meaningful work to me because very few of our Hometown Diplomats looked like me, and helping people find their own unique paths—perhaps through the Foreign Service—truly energized me. While I knew the Foreign Service would not be the path for me for much longer, my belief in the agency and its purpose and mission never wavered then, and nor has it wavered since.

I believe that if we are to continue to influence and strengthen our work, we must continually bring diverse voices, perspectives, and lived experiences into the fold, and at no time is that diversity more critical than during times of turmoil. That we were at war was known to all, and I painted a realistic picture of my work and what serving entailed. The Foreign Service is not just a job or a career path; it is a lifestyle. I believe people are capable of making their own choices when provided with the necessary information to do so.

The second key program launched by Secretary Powell was a task force charged with building a five-year plan for the continuation of the diversification of the Foreign Service. Secretary Powell believed that, as with the military, the body of FSOs should be reflective of the greater diversity and representation of American society, and it wasn't. The diplomatic corps at that time was still primarily white males of higher socioeconomic status.

The secretary's diversification of the Foreign Service wasn't just about gender, race, and ethnicity. It was about a true reflection of the American people, and that included diversification of socioeconomic status and which pockets of the US people were recruited from. Because the Pickering Fellowship was one of the models that would be used, they included some Pickering alumni on one of the subcommittees to provide insight into the program's structure, lessons learned, and successes, and I was excited to be part of the process.

The idea that this leader, Secretary Powell, who did not have to consider how to diversify the Foreign Service chose to intentionally do so was as inspiring as it was powerful. He asked the committee for recommendations grounded in data and experiences of what worked. Our recommendations would form the basis of the next five years of recruitment strategies for the State Department. Secretary Powell wanted structures and strategies in place that allowed for accountability and visible progress—another inspirational move.

As simple as that may all sound, we know it doesn't happen a lot. Secretary Powell was true to his word. He listened, assigned tasks, and held people accountable. He influenced structures and systems to systemically and intentionally create sustainable opportunities to diversify our recruits for years to come.

Being part of these two programs relit a spark in me. I wanted to be the catalyst who opened doors. I wanted to be the catalyst for the young DeAngelas. The catalyst for young people in the Midwest or in the South. The catalyst for that young Black girl, Black boy, or Latino. The catalyst for low-income, first-generation kids, most of whom would never dream that they could go to Stanford or Princeton, go into the Foreign Service, or speak multiple languages. I wanted to be the catalyst because I could see their potential. I knew that when you connected those students with potential opportunities and access, they would soar. I knew because I had been one of those students.

This experience would push me to think about how my own journey of exploration began. So, in the spring of 2004, I began to explore higher education opportunities, and I landed a job as assistant director of admission at my alma mater, Stanford. I was excited, but I also wasn't ready to separate myself completely from my Foreign Service life. My love and passion for the Foreign Service was second only to Stanford. With my acceptance into the prestigious Pickering Fellowship at nineteen, a career in the Foreign Service was everything that I had prepared myself to do with my degrees in international relations and international policy. I had grown up in the Foreign Service, and I had thrived in it. Ambassador Davis believed in me, mentored me, and envisioned me as an ambassador or in a higher position one day. I was on a trajectory of success, and people had expectations for me and had invested in me. Departing was an unsettling feeling, so I chose to take a one-year leave without pay. This provided me with the opportunity to come back and continue my Foreign Service career if I found that a path in higher education was not right for me.

My decision to return to Stanford had been a unilateral one, and I had assumed my brother would come to California with Kelly and me, but Jason chose to remain in DC. Jason and I talked about that transition years later, and I realized that I could have handled it better. I had encouraged him to uproot his life and come live with me in DC, and then, less than a year later, before he'd had time to put down new roots, I decided to up and leave. I felt guilty when Jason decided to stay, knowing it would be hard on him, and I felt selfish for making the decision to leave DC.

Those first thoughts of being selfish around my choices and my career, which had begun when I was so many miles away from Granny when she died, would continue to show up in various pockets of my life. Over the years, I would never be able to stop myself from questioning my decisions, but I would learn to work through the feelings associated with those decisions.

On our last day in DC, Kelly and I helped Jason move into his new apartment. Jason had lived on his own before coming to DC and was more than capable, but I felt responsible for leaving my little brother, so I ran back and forth to the store that day, buying kitchen items, towels, sheets—anything and everything I thought he could use. It was a bittersweet moment as we hugged and laughed at the curb of his new place before Kelly and I said our goodbyes.

I was proud of Jason for standing his ground, and I am continually inspired by the amazing life he has built for himself in DC. That year of living together was the first time we had spent any length of time together as adults, and it strengthened our relationship. The kid who was my pesky little brother became one of my best friends and my biggest champion. I'm the big sis, but the truth is that he has carried me through some challenging times, and he has been an incredible role model for my son since the day X was born.

He's also the person I call when I want to do something crazy because he's always up for crazy!

The following morning, Kelly and I headed to California. I was running on pure adrenaline with the excitement of returning to what I consider my second home of Stanford and the Bay. Kelly seemed excited for what was next, but honestly, I don't know if we truly talked about what he was feeling or if he had any worries. My decision to return to Stanford really had been a unilateral one. Staying with the parents of my college best friend, Alison, would help our transition to the Bay go smoothly, and we arrived in the beautiful sunshine of the Bay filled with hope and possibility. This new beginning would bring us our greatest joy and our darkest moments.

CHAPTER 13
I HOPE YOU DANCE

"I Hope You Dance"

... and when you get the choice to sit it out or dance
I hope you dance

—Lee Ann Womack

hen I stepped back onto Stanford's campus in the fall of 2004, this time as a professional, it felt like coming home. The beauty of Stanford reminded me that I could be anything and do anything. It reminded me that I didn't have one path or one choice; I could reinvent myself as many times as I wanted because I had the skill set to do so. When I stepped into my role in the Office of Undergraduate Admission at Stanford, all my fears about how and what I would transition to and how it might affect the trajectory of my career evaporated. The ability to see and create an impact was instantly clear to me—the *what are we doing* and *why are we doing it* just fell into place.

I was eager and energetic, and I knew the impact that I wanted to have. I was also new to the field, and as a result, I made a few missteps in those early days. Fortunately, just as I had amazing mentors in the Foreign Service, I also had them at Stanford. Dr. V. Joy Simmons was one of those early Stanford mentors. I met her shortly after I arrived in the Office of Undergraduate Admission. Joy gave me the confidence to be my authentic self because she always showed up authentically. She didn't tone down who she was or what her passions or commitments were. This slender woman, with her light caramel complexion, embodied strength and class. She was dressed, as they used to say, to the nines every time. As she was blazing a trail in her role as a radiologist with Kaiser Permanente, she was also, as a trustee of Stanford, demanding to know what the university was doing about Black student enrollment. "I want to know about the Jacksons and the Johnsons," she would say. "Are they getting in, and are they graduating?" She was unapologetically Black and unapologetically focused on creating access and opportunity for Black students.

At one point, Joy requested a meeting to go over the data of Black students. Because my role involved working with the recruitment of Black students, I began putting the data together for the meeting and then provided it to my boss, the acting dean of admission, Anna Marie Porras, for review. Anna Marie was a beautiful, petite, and powerful Latina with an amazing soul and a quiet yet commanding presence. She had a crispness to the way she dressed, and she'd always walk into a meeting with her red notebook in hand, in which she took meticulous notes. It was the power she exuded through her calmness and deep thoughtfulness that drew me in, and I immediately saw her as someone I wanted to emulate. But first, she would frustrate me.

After she reviewed the report I had put together for Joy, she tore it apart as if I were straight out of college and didn't know how to put a presentation together. In true Anna Marie fashion, though, she tore it apart calmly, quietly, and kindly. I remember thinking, *Just because I haven't been in admissions and don't know admissions speak or how you all think doesn't mean I'm stupid.* I was so frustrated, but I went back, I pulled the data differently, and I redid the briefing book. Then she and I met to review it again.

I can still so clearly see us seated at the long oak table in the conference room across the hall from our offices in Old Union. Old Union, with its sandstone walls and red clay roof, was one of the buildings on campus that everyone knew. Just beyond the courtyard stood the campus's famous fountain known as The Claw. Outside, students rolled by on bikes and skateboards, unaware of the standoff happening inside. It was just Anna Marie and me sitting at the end of the table, and she went through the briefing book without a word. She, of course, had her little red notebook with her, and when she finished reviewing my presentation, she wrote two things in that red notebook, closed it, and then slid my presentation binder back across the table to me. "You're ready. Right?"

I said, "Yes." And that was it.

It wasn't until several years later that Anna Marie revealed the lesson she was trying to teach me: "What I needed you to understand and bring in that moment was not just your passion, love, and understanding of your community. I needed you to understand and know the difference in how you show up as an expert about your community."

Anna Marie was another one of my amazing Stanford mentors who taught me so much. I'm not as quiet and soft in my approach as Anna Marie, but I try to carry her quiet thoughtfulness and patience in how I approach certain circumstances. Still today—particularly after losing her to cancer in January of 2015—when I am at the table talking about policy, data, and the shaping of our practices, I often feel like Anna Marie is at my shoulder, guiding me. In those moments, I often ask myself, *What would Anna Marie do?*

Anna Marie would serve as acting dean of admission in my first year of working in Stanford admission. When they closed the search for the permanent dean of admission position, it was not Anna Marie who would fill that seat. Anna Marie was a Stanford alum who had been working at Stanford since 1991. She served as a beacon of strength and hope for women and students of color, and her work in admission reflected that. But the university was looking for something different at that time, and they would fill the position of dean of admission with a man from a peer institution, who had a more traditional admissions experience and name-brand appeal.

I don't presume to know all the factors that led to such a decision or to know whether it was the right decision for Stanford. I can only speak to how it felt to me. I had loved my time as a student at Stanford, and I loved the work I was now part of in admission. Much of that love came from the opportunity to move within a space that believed in women who looked like me: young, dynamic women of color who were grounded in this institution. To me, this change in leadership felt like a betrayal. In my eyes, it signaled a shift was on the horizon—a shift in the very space that had grounded me and had felt so much like home to me from the moment I had stepped foot on its campus so many years ago.

Anna Marie would go on to do more amazing things for Stanford in other capacities, but she would not lead admission again. That was hard for me. After a year under the new dean, I would be offered the position of assistant dean of undergraduate admission. It was not an easy decision for me—I had just spent the past year jumping through hoops to prove the value of my work and trying to figure out if Stanford was still where I belonged. But I believed in the difference we were making and needed to continue to make. When I accepted the position, it was the inspiration of mentors such as Ambassador Davis, Dr. Joy Simmons, and Anna Marie Porras that gave me the strength and confidence to make it clear to my new boss that if I accepted the position, I would continue to be exactly who I had been. I would continue to passionately advocate for access for all the students who historically did not have access, and I would continue to challenge the status quo and him. And I did.

We began to really dig into our outreach work and think about how we were diversifying our student body, how we were reaching new parts of the country, and how we were showing up differently. I realized that because we had this reputation of being elitist, we didn't recruit in certain places. We weren't present at certain conferences, and there were spaces we just weren't showing up in. I began asking my peers and leadership, people who had been in admission longer than I had been, "What are we trying to do? What is the outcome we are trying to achieve?" So often, they didn't have answers to those questions, and when they did, I could see that what they were doing wasn't going to work.

This was when I began to really think about systemic change and to understand that the power of an individual dynamic leader is wonderful, but if the work and impact are tied to that individual leader, who can come and go, how can true social and systemic change really happen? From that point forward, when I would train my officers, we would come together to think and talk about what structures we needed to put in place, what data should always be given and why, and how we could change the landscape using the technology, network, and policies and procedures that were part of how we did admission work.

We challenged how we recruited, how we selected students, and who we hired. My impassioned challenges were not just for the good of the institution; they were for the mission of who we were. I was responsible for ensuring that we were the inclusive, diverse, and rich environment that we said we were. I pushed and challenged my team to understand what an inclusive, diverse, and rich environment even looked like.

Together, my team and I would embark on an outreach tour like nothing we had ever done before. Our recruiters were connected to the communities of low-income, first-generation families, students with disabilities, African Americans, Latinx, Native Americans, Asian Americans, and LGBTQ individuals. As a group of diverse recruiters ourselves, we would go into the communities, who could see themselves in us, and we would begin the conversations that would demystify the admission process for those students. It was our mission to let the students in communities that Stanford recruiters had not historically reached out to know that they, too, could and should be applying to the likes of Stanford, Princeton, and MIT.

While the work remained incredibly meaningful and purposeful, the shift I had experienced within Stanford's leadership had created a shift in how I began to move through the world professionally. I wasn't sure Stanford was the same for me at that moment. That same year, I would experience what felt like another betrayal.

That betrayal would be a very personal one, and it rocked the sense of home I felt in yet another sacred space in my life: my marriage. I can't or won't fully describe the feeling of that betrayal, but I can tell you that when I allowed myself to really wade into that space, it felt dark, it felt cold, and it felt soundless. Too often, we suffer through this type of pain alone. Sometimes, it's because we feel like we must be strong, because we feel ashamed, or because we simply don't know what else to do. Sometimes, it is all those things all at once.

There were many moments when I asked myself what I could have done differently and how I could have stopped it from happening. And most painfully, I wanted to know why—why I was betrayed in this way. Along my journey, I've gained clarity on the last question: One, I will never understand the why, and it may never be for me to understand. And two, it wasn't about me; it was about their choice not to honor what we had.

Having my trust shaken in two of the most sacred spaces in my life changed me. I began to approach life with more caution. I didn't stop trusting all things, but I began to gradually close myself off and to deepen my coping mechanism of compartmentalizing my feelings. I forged a boundary between the different aspects of my life, and that included keeping my professional and personal lives extremely separate.

The depth of my compartmentalization would show itself over the next few years, culminating shortly after I achieved my dream of becoming Dr. DeAngela Burns-Wallace.

CHAPTER 14

LOSE YOURSELF

"Lose Yourself"

The moment, you own it, you better never let it go (Go)
You only get one shot, do not miss your chance to blow
This opportunity comes once in a lifetime

—Eminem

In January 2008, while in my roles as both assistant dean and new doctoral student, I found myself with flu-like symptoms persistent enough to warrant a visit to the doctor. The doctor would surprise me not with antibiotics but with a "you're pregnant" announcement. And it truly was a surprise because Kelly and I had been trying unsuccessfully for a few years. When I enrolled in the doctoral program, I had decided that I would continue to work on my marriage during this time and then, once I graduated, I would, one, come to a decision about the future of my marriage and, two, look into the possibility of adoption.

Even with all the uncertainty in my life, I was incredibly excited when my doctor gave me the news. Even the challenge of cross-country travel between my work at Stanford and my doctoral program at the University of Pennsylvania (UPenn) could not dampen my excitement. I did know, however, that I would need to be concerned about the impact my news would have on my status in the program. This executive doctoral program was still relatively young, and the school was highly invested in making sure our small cohort of twenty-four completed the program on time and at the same caliber as its full-time doctoral students. Leadership was under a lot of scrutiny, and I believed if the people in charge knew about my pregnancy, they would question my ability to complete the program—and they did.

Given the level of my coursework and commitment that I had already demonstrated, I shouldn't have had to worry about how my pregnancy might impact the leadership's perception of whether I could continue at the same level, but that is the reality for women in many environments. I know a lot of women, particularly those working on the corporate side, who have had to question, *What does it mean if I have children and I want to take time out of work? How will that impact my career trajectory?* In that moment, I wanted to share my wonderful news, and it was so hard feeling like I couldn't simply because others would then judge my competence.

I wondered, *Are they going to try to push me out? What does that look like? How do I position myself better?* In the end, it was about holding on to my own power to determine my future for as long as possible. So, I strategized how to make that happen.

Once you complete the coursework and pass your qualifying exam, you are a doctoral candidate, and it's a lot harder to kick out a candidate. So, I didn't tell anybody in my executive doctoral program about my pregnancy until after I had passed my qualifying exams. And even at that juncture, members of the faculty felt the need to question, debate, and decide if they should make me pause until after my child was born to complete my dissertation. I wasn't in the room for that conversation, and I am thankful for my mentors who were and who fought for me. I was allowed to continue in my program with no delays.

By the time I finished my qualifying exam, proposal defense, and all the necessary prep work, it was early September, and my doctor put me on bed rest for what would be the last month of my pregnancy. I had my dissertation to finish, and I kept telling my son, *Don't you come yet. Mama's got three more interviews, Mama's got two more interviews, Mama's got one more interview.* I finished my interviews and sent them off for transcription on Sunday, October 5. The following Tuesday, my water broke, and off we rushed to the hospital—Kelly, me, and my parents, who, as planned, had arrived in advance of my delivery.

I do not manage the *anticipation* of potential physical pain well and am known to freak out a bit in those moments. So, while I was incredibly excited to have my baby, my mind kept spinning about how incredibly painful it was all going to be. And, of course, it was. It was also long and hard, and in the end, it would turn into a C-section delivery. I was so grateful for my doula, Dena, who, as an undergrad at Stanford, had worked with me in admission. Dena was amazing, talking me down from my I-don't-think-I-can-do-this panic attacks and walking me through everything that was going on. I am not sure I would have survived without her. A quick side note here: I didn't know or understand the power of doulas until Dena, one of my mentees, introduced it to me. Never underestimate whom you can learn from on your journey.

My parents had also been in the birthing room with us throughout, but when the decision for a C-section was made, I had to leave them behind as I was brought into the operating room with Kelly by my side. When I was wheeled back into the hall with my baby cradled in my arms, my parents were there, waiting to meet their grandson. The immense swell of joy I felt when I first laid eyes on Xavier was perfectly matched by the profound peace that washed over me as my parents stood beside us.

I cannot express the meaning of my parents' presence and unwavering support during that period in my life. The upheaval in my marriage at that time was not new. We—or maybe it was already just me by that point, I'm honestly not sure—were still trying to mend and strengthen our marriage when my pregnancy surprised us. My parents being there meant I wouldn't be alone in the joy and the care of my newborn. My dad would head home the following week to return to work, and my mom would stay with us, helping Xavier and me find our rhythm, through the end of October.

I must digress for a moment to share that my beautiful son, Xavier, was born on my brother's birthday and why that bit of fate is so ironic. Xavier looks just like my brother. It's the craziest thing when family members see them together. My aunt even said, "It looked like Jason spit him out, not you." And it's my brother's fault they share a birthday. When I was pregnant, Jason kept telling me my son had to be born in September so that I would have to share my birthday month—because Jason had no intention of sharing his birthday month. I can still hear him say, "You're going to have this baby in September, Dee, and share *your* birthday month with *your* child." I would have been fine with it, but Jason jinxed himself. Not only does he share his birthday month, but he also shares the day. Clearly, we are serious about our birthdays. (We really do celebrate the full month!) My son was born at ten in the morning on my brother's birthday, twenty-nine years apart, and they have been linked ever since. Sharing the same birthday is their special bond.

Between November of 2008 and March of 2009, Xavier and I spent much of our time on the couch as he slept and breastfed in my lap while I balanced my laptop (yup, also in my lap) and moved between writing my dissertation and reading and scoring applications of high school students eager to attend Stanford in the fall. The winter months are Stanford's "reading" months when we review applications, and that was work I could thankfully do from home. During that period, I would also travel to UPenn once a month for my in-person doctoral coursework. My parents once again came to my rescue. X and I would fly to Kansas City so I could drop him off at my parents', and then I would fly to UPenn for my coursework and back to Kansas City to pick him up. Then the two of us would return home to California.

I defended my dissertation in March. (Yes, I delivered a child and a dissertation within five months of each other!) And yes, I had put the work in, but I also had someone in that room who carried my name and said, "This woman right here, if you're going to bet on anybody who could finish, you bet on her." That person was the faculty advisor, Dr. Shaun Harper. Maybe it's something that I should have simply expected that he would and should do, but there is a part of me that has come to assume that people won't always go to bat for you unless they have something to gain. While countless people have been there for me throughout my life without thought of personal gain, I have learned that it is not guaranteed, so I often don't allow myself to rely on others in that way.

But Dr. Harper did, unequivocally, have my back. He was my champion, stepping out with faith and confidence in me when others would not. There was never a thought in my mind, or in his, that I was going to pause or defer or not complete the program. It was the combination of me knowing I could do it and being supported by those who chose to see who I was and how I showed up that got me through.

Not only did I finish on time, but I finished with distinction. And then my life fell apart.

CHAPTER 15
NO MORE DRAMA

"No More Drama"

I don't know, only God knows where the story ends for me,
but I know where the story begins.
It's up to us to choose whether we win or lose, and I choose to win.

—Mary J. Blige

One evening, about a month after I defended my dissertation, I picked my son up from daycare and headed home. As I parked in front of our apartment in the East Bay, the sun had almost set, and when I opened my car door, the wintery chill in the air caught me by surprise. I grabbed my bag and then scooped Xavier out of his infant car seat in the back. Xavier was about six months old, and I remember jostling him on my hip as I unlocked the door of our apartment. I remember these details because when I opened the door and flicked on the lights, nothing happened. I stepped into the darkness and flicked another switch—still nothing. I became aware of how cold it was—cold like the heat hadn't been working for hours.

I quickly shut the door and leaned my back against it. Hugging Xavier to my chest, I knew I could no longer keep pretending that everything was OK, and yet I did on many fronts. But first, I would receive a call from a new friend, whom I would come to call my "later-in-life bestie," Antoinette. I cannot remember why she happened to call in that moment, but when I heard her voice, my facade crumbled, and through my tears, I just kept saying, "I don't know what to do; I don't know what to do."

Antoinette was my angel who came to my rescue, emotionally and financially. She arranged for X and me to stay at a hotel for a couple of nights until I could get my power turned back on. I cannot recall if I even knew where my husband was at the time or if I had been able to reach him, but the next morning, I got myself ready for work and X ready to go to daycare. Together, we headed out the hotel door as if it were any other ordinary day.

There I was, the successful and confident assistant dean of undergraduate admission at Stanford University, and I had arrived home the previous evening to find that my utilities had been shut off for nonpayment. By this time, my ability to compartmentalize my emotions and the different aspects of my life was second nature. I remember going back to work the next day, committed to maintaining the pretense that my life was running smoothly because, honestly, how do you share, and whom do you share with when you've been appearing to be so together for so long?

I had to face that it was time for me to make some life-altering decisions. When my son was born, I felt such an amazing swell of joy. And in that moment, I realized that somewhere along the way, I had lost the joy of who I was in my life. With X, God gave me my joy back, and I had sworn I wouldn't let anyone take it from me again, and yet here I was. Even though I was still married, I was alone in this, and it was time I accepted that truth. I needed to do whatever it took to make it right for my son, even if it meant moving back to the very place I couldn't wait to get away from when I was younger.

My family and lifelong friends were in Kansas City, and my son and I needed to be surrounded by their love and support. I graduated from my EdD program in May 2009, and that same month, I submitted my resignation, agreeing to stay on at Stanford through the end of August to help with the summer recruitment cycle. I sent my son to stay with my parents in Kansas City, and over the next three months, I flew back and forth to Kansas City every other Friday to be with him and for the occasional job interview, and then I flew back to California on Sunday.

My time in California during those months was filled with working, packing, and getting my life in order. I didn't have a job in Kansas City yet, but I didn't care because I knew that I could not stay in California in the middle of what had come to feel like madness. If taking care of X meant I needed to return to my childhood home, where we would live in my parents' basement, that's what we would do. At the time, I told my husband that X and I were going home, and it didn't matter to me whether he decided to come or not. In between work and packing that summer, I was applying for jobs, and by mid-August, I had secured a job at UM.

While I knew what I had to do, it was still a difficult move for me. I never intended to move back home. I felt like it wasn't the place for me. I wanted to do and see more than I thought Missouri had to offer. Growing up in Kansas City, I always felt different, like I never truly belonged beyond the bounds of my family. And when I went to Stanford, it was the first place where, like my dad said, I found my people, and I never looked back.

I had lived all over the world at that point. I spoke multiple languages. I had met and worked for the likes of Secretary Powell, President Mandela, President Carter, and Secretary Albright. I had been all over China and South Africa and all across Asia and Europe, and here I was, heading back home to Missouri.

The move back was made more difficult because I also felt like I had failed. I hadn't been able to make my marriage work. And even though my husband and I had gone through couples counseling, I had done everything I could to try to make it work, and I knew separating was the right decision for my son and me, I still felt like a failure. My faith is a big part of who I am. My wedding had ended with "what God joins together, let no man put asunder," and we had pledged "til death do us part." I had meant every word. I struggled for a long time with being in a marriage that clearly was not working but believing that I was supposed to figure it out, stick it out, and never discuss our failure openly. It was not healthy.

After I was settled back in Missouri, I went back to therapy—this time, for myself. Therapy helped me understand that it was OK for me to fail in this space and that I needed to mourn the loss of my ten-year marriage and the relationship that my husband and I had created together for almost twenty years. No matter how much time passes, my marriage will always be an important part of my story and a necessary one, and I am thankful for it. In the fall of 2010, the time had come for me to figure out my life as a divorced single parent.

As X and I were enveloped in the fold of family and friends, I came to realize that moving back home was the best thing that could have happened to us. Coming back to this region did two things for me. It grounded me with family and friends who supported me through everything. And my past experiences in so many other environments brought a richness to the environments that I joined back here in this region. It allowed me to develop an appreciation for this region that I grew up in and could now see in a very different way. I could see how to pour into it, grow from it, and ground myself in it.

This new stage of my life enabled me to live near my family, continue my work in higher education, and get on a plane and continue to fulfill my numerous responsibilities and engagements around the country. I could make all those things happen and still create a home and a foundation that allowed X to grow up surrounded by family. Coming home to this region saved me. Coming home propelled me, my family, and my career in ways I could not have imagined, and I will be forever grateful for home.

CHAPTER 16
COUNT ON ME

"Count on Me"

Count on me through thick and thin
A friendship that will never end
When you are weak I will be strong
Helping you to carry on

—Whitney Houston and CeCe Winans

y new position as assistant vice provost and director of access initiatives in the Division of Enrollment Management at MU was in Columbia, two hours away from my parents' home in Kansas City, Missouri. We wouldn't be living in their basement after all, but I still needed to find a home for X and me and a daycare for him that I could trust. Between Columbia and Kansas City, there is this small town called Boonville.

Boonville was a town I used to tag along to with Marshaun, my best friend since seventh grade, when she and her family would go visit her family there. We would hang out with her cousins and have adventures outside of the city. Marshaun's family; her mom, Miss Samantha; and her Aunt Ritta became my family. So, when I needed daycare for X, it made sense that he would go to Aunt Ritta's daycare and be with people I felt comfortable entrusting him to.

Monday through Friday, every morning, I would drive X the sixty-mile round trip from Columbia to Boonville and then back to Columbia to begin my day at the university. Then I did the same thing each night. There was many a night that I couldn't make it down that highway. I was at work, I was tired, or a meeting ran late. There were all kinds of challenges, and Aunt Ritta would say, "Girl, I'm going to take this boy on home and feed him. You go on and do what you got to do and come get him when you need to." That's how it was. If X needed to stay, I packed his overnight bag, and he stayed over with Aunt Ritta.

If I needed to bring X early or late, Aunt Ritta was always willing to help. I remember driving up and down I-70 so many times, crossing this old rickety bridge between Columbia and Boonville that always made me nervous. On Fridays after work, I would have our bags in the car when I picked up X from Aunt Ritta's, and then he and I would make the long drive to my parents' home in Kansas City. We'd hang out for the weekend and head back early Monday morning, dropping X off at Aunt Ritta's on my way back to the university.

We did that schedule for almost three years until X was ready for preschool. And then I found a beautiful preschool in Columbia run by Miss Joanne, who would then carry him forward. In the years that we were in Columbia, I had so much support from Marshaun, Aunt

Ritta, my parents, Jason, and so many of my childhood girlfriends, who would make the two-hour drive to visit, to help us celebrate any occasion, or just to stay over.

My early years in Columbia were just the beginning of the many times they would all support me in this in-between world. I traveled back and forth so much in those days, and when X came to school age, my parents would then carry the heavy load of traveling back and forth to Columbia, coming to be part of the activities he was involved in, and staying with him when my work required me to travel.

The most beautiful part of everyone's support and love was that they all just offered, no questions asked. All that love and support allowed me to continue what would become my life's work of championing equal access, opportunity, and representation for all.

After four years on campus, during the 2013–14 academic year, the provost nominated me for the emerging leaders fellowship program of the American Council on Education (ACE). The fellowship is a one-year, full-time placement at another higher education institution. It provides the fellow with the opportunity to shadow higher education presidents, provosts, and other senior leaders to observe how their institutions address strategic planning, resource allocation, institutional advancement, policy advocacy, and other challenges.

Most fellows utilize this opportunity to participate in an institution in another area of the country, but that wasn't going to work for me. I had moved back to Missouri so that my son would be surrounded by the support and love of family. He was still so young at five years old, and I couldn't imagine moving him far away. I also couldn't imagine not taking advantage of this prestigious national fellowship and the value of learning from another president or provost. I had some brainstorming to do about how I could find a fellowship placement that would continue to provide X with the solid foundation of family that I wanted for him and be of value to my life's work.

A colleague encouraged me to think outside the box for a solution. I needed to be at a different institution where I could learn from a dynamic and impactful leader. I didn't have to go far or someplace obscure. I could find that dynamic organization in my own backyard—or my parents' backyard, I should say. I chose KU, just thirty minutes from my parents. I packed all my stuff up and put it in storage, and X and I moved into my parents' basement for our first, but not our last, time.

Spending a year under the tutelage of Chancellor Bernadette Gray-Little was life-changing. I marveled at how she, serving as the first woman and first African American chancellor at KU from 2009 to 2017, addressed her detractors with grace while courageously moving KU beyond what anyone thought possible.

Chancellor Gray-Little invested in the institution in new and different pockets that enabled the university to impact student success intentionally and strategically, and she challenged everyone to a higher level of excellence every day. I remember one meeting in which a new leader was presenting their first ninety-day report. Everyone was in a celebratory mood and full of congratulations. While Chancellor Gray-Little did give praise, at that moment, she also unequivocally challenged that individual to push further. Chancellor Gray-Little would push me further at various stages in my career and, to this day, still takes the time to call and congratulate me when I reach those milestones. In later years, she would be my lead nominator for membership in the Council on Foreign Relations.

It is the leaders and mentors like Chancellor Gray-Little who make you believe that you can succeed in the spaces and places you may have once thought unattainable and who make you understand your responsibility to pay that belief forward to the leaders coming behind you.

I would return to KU a few years after my fellowship and have the honor of helping the university reach the level of excellence that Chancellor Gray-Little envisioned. But first, I would return to MU and apply the knowledge and tools I had gathered in my fellowship for the success of our students in Columbia, Missouri. Surprisingly, I would do so in a new role as assistant vice provost for undergraduate studies.

Halfway through my fellowship, I was at an ACE conference and asked the provost at MU, who had recommended me for the fellowship program, if he would have a cup of coffee with me. I let him know that I had been informed that I might not have a position at MU after I finished my fellowship and that I needed to know if he was willing to sign the release so I could find a new position. His face went blank.

"What are you talking about?"

I then shared with him the recent meeting I had with my MU supervisor, in which she explained to me my MU responsibilities that I had either not done completely or not done to her satisfaction when I was engaged with my fellowship and throughout my history under her leadership. When higher education institutions sign off on a fellowship, they release the fellows from their home institution responsibilities for the year while continuing to pay their salaries, with the intent that the fellows return and share with their home institutions the knowledge they gained through the fellowship experiences.

For that reason, fellows are *not allowed* to job hunt during their fellowships. And now, my MU supervisor was suggesting that my presence wasn't necessary and that, upon further reflection, I had acted with incompetence or insubordination while in my role. There were politics and dynamics between the provost and my vice provost that I was unaware of at the time, which prompted some of this reaction to me. I told the provost, as I had my supervisor, that if MU didn't want or need me anymore, then I welcomed opportunities from other institutions, but I needed his release so I could explore those options. He had no knowledge of my recent conversations, and most importantly, he made clear that he did not agree with her assessment. My path would shift that day, setting me on a path that would lead me back home for good.

CHAPTER 17

YOU'VE GOT A FRIEND

"You've Got a Friend"

Winter, spring, summer or fall
All you have to do is call
And I'll be there

—Carole King

“Well, Dr. Burns-Wallace, you ready to come work for me?”

Dr. Jim Spain, vice provost for undergraduate studies at MU, had asked me this question many times over the past few years, and I would always reply, “Dr. Spain, I love what I do. I'm good. We're working together.”

And he would reply, “All right, but you let me know when you're coming to work for me, Dr. Burns-Wallace.”

“All right, Dr. Spain, I will,” I'd say, and we'd both laugh.

An agricultural professor by training, Dr. Spain specialized in cows, and he would often open a conversation with "I'm a brown-cow, green-grass, and white-milk kind of guy. That's all I know." Dr. Spain and I met when I first came to MU and worked in enrollment management. Student access and early outreach were under my purview at the time, and his office was a partner office that handled undergraduate education and student success. We worked very closely together and had a great relationship—which is why he always asked when I was coming to work for him.

From the beginning, Dr. Spain always called me Dr. Burns-Wallace, and I always called him Dr. Spain. It was a personal endearment founded on a deep level of mutual respect. It was important to Jim that no one dropped my title or acted with any disrespect toward me when he was around—a sentiment and action I deeply appreciated.

This time, Dr. Spain's question, *Dr. Burns-Wallace, are you ready to come work for me?* had been prompted by my conversation with the MU provost just two days earlier, and I was happy to reply, "Yes, Dr. Spain, I am." That invitation from Jim would keep me at MU just a bit longer.

When I returned from my ACE fellowship at KU in June of 2014, X and I moved back to Columbia, and over the next several months, we settled ourselves back into our life there. I became fully engaged in my role of assistant vice provost, which Dr. Spain had created for me, and I began to think about buying a house for X and me.

Dr. Spain would empower me to combine all I had learned at MU in my previous role as assistant vice provost of enrollment management and through my ACE fellowship to build the infrastructure to transform student success at MU. This would serve as the foundation for the work that I would later do when I returned to the KU. But the most powerful step Dr. Spain took was to say, "Do what you need to do, however you need to do it, and tell me who I need to talk to to get you what you need to be successful for our students." At every turn, he would support. At every turn, he would listen. At every turn, he would empower me as a person, me as a leader, and me as an educator.

In every action he took, Jim reinforced what Judy Moon had taught me years earlier: Be humble enough to say, "I'm already here. I already have the title. I need you to do it. I want to help you grow. I want to help you shine."

Dr. Spain brought me into rooms that he didn't need to bring me into. He would tell me that my voice and perspective needed to be heard in those rooms. He always made me feel like we were on equal footing and that we were in this together.

Dr. Spain is a tall white man, and I can still see him standing in my doorway, saying to me with a smile, "So, Dr. Burns-Wallace, what are we getting into today?"

Everything we got into didn't always work, but even in those moments, Jim's support and belief in me never wavered. He'd simply say, "OK, Dr. Burns-Wallace, what are we going to do now?" I learned so much from the humanity of who he was. He would always, always take the time to listen. I honestly don't know how he got anything done because no matter who knocked on his door, he would stop and, in his big booming voice, say, "Come on in and take a seat."

Dr. Spain invested in me, and together, we accomplished so much. It was at MU that I began my work around the financial barriers unrelated to tuition that were impeding student graduation. By leveraging technologies, we were able to implement systems and structures that provided a deeper insight into the success of our students. MU was an environment in which we were able to test data, systems, and structures related to student success, but most importantly, MU offered the space in which in-depth collaboration could flourish.

Big campuses like MU, KU, and Stanford are highly decentralized. The work within the various schools, colleges, and programs in those individual universities is all pulling toward the same goals, but they often go about it in different ways. Over my next two years at MU, we worked to identify and bring together the key people and partners from the various areas of the institution that impacted student success so that we could understand how each area was functioning. From there, we were able to map out where the gaps existed, particularly for our marginalized students, and begin restructuring our processes and procedures to fill those gaps. By helping all students progress and graduate at higher levels, we began to level the playing field, particularly for our students of color.

The knowledge I gained from my fellowship at KU and my work with Dr. Spain would serve as the foundation that would accelerate my work in student success in my (yet unknown to me) future position as vice provost for undergraduate education at KU.

In the spring of 2015, on a visit to my parents in Kansas City, I decided to stop in at KU to catch up with everyone. When I arrived at KU for my visit, one of the first people I met with was the interim provost. It wasn't long before she told me, "You know, we're ready to hire the vice provost for undergraduate education."

This was a role that had been created shortly before I had begun my fellowship there. I had helped think through some of the pieces of that position because we were doing similar work at MU that had shown impactful results, so I was very familiar with the role. My response was, "That's great."

"You need to apply," she said.

I replied, "They are not going to give that role to a nonfaculty member at KU. I know that y'all believe in faculty being in those roles that control curriculum—period."

"No, you need to apply."

I left it at that, and later that afternoon, when I was visiting with Chancellor Little-Gray, she asked me if the interim provost had talked to me about the vice provost of undergraduate education position. "Yes, ma'am," I said.

"And," she said, "what is your hesitation?"

I explained to her my concern that I would not be seriously considered as a candidate because I did not come from a tenured track background; I was considered an administrator, not faculty.

"I would not be telling you to consider applying if you would not be given a fair and competitive shot as a candidate" was her response. And that was that.

I applied, interviewed, and was slated to begin my tenure as vice provost for undergraduate education at KU in January of 2016. I would be the Dr. Spain at KU; he had helped shape and encourage my journey, and I would be forever grateful as I prepared to transition. But in the months leading up to my transition from MU to KU, I would witness the courage and strength of the students of color at MU and would take those lessons with me.

CHAPTER 18
FIGHT THE POWER

"Fight the Power"

Our freedom of speech is freedom or death
We got to fight the powers that be

—Public Enemy

The assistant to the provost called and asked me to join a meeting that was currently in progress. I put aside what I was doing and headed across MU's administrative building, slicing through the tension-filled air that had been building momentum over the past several months. As I entered the large outer office where the assistant to the provost sat, I said, "Hello," and followed her directions to enter the provost's conference room.

Gathered in deep conversation around the provost's small conference table sat five or six people, all of whom I knew and worked with on a regular basis. Although I did not initially wonder why I was in the room with these individuals, I did begin to take in that all of them were either cabinet members or vice provost–level and above. I was the only one not at that level. Later, I would also register that I was the only Black person in the room. It was Dr. Spain who had brought my name into that room and who invited me to sit down and brought me up to speed on their conversation.

"Dr. Burns-Wallace, we're trying to prepare how to best respond to the ongoing protest and now the hunger strike. We are not," he made clear, "trying to stop the protest. What we want is to ensure we are providing the students with what they need to be safe while they exercise their right to bring their voice to issues that matter to them. We need to understand what questions we need to be asking in support of the students; how we, as members of the administration, navigate a student boycott against the administration; and in what ways we can take action to help resolve the issues."

Now, let me share with you the momentous circumstances that enveloped the campus of MU during that time and that led to the strategy session.

In the fall of 2015, racial tensions on campus escalated to extreme levels. Tensions had been high since the August 9, 2014, murder of eighteen-year-old Michael Brown by police in Ferguson, Missouri. After Brown's murder, MU's administration held town halls to provide students, faculty, and staff with space to process the tragedy in Ferguson and its implications for the broader Missouri community. During various town halls in the fall of 2014 and spring of 2015, tensions continued to climb when several students challenged then-Chancellor R. Bowen Loftin on what they perceived as the administration's inadequate response to systemic racism.

I do believe that in providing these spaces for dialogue, the administration was trying to do the right thing. But much like what my family and I, and my Black peers and their families, had experienced in response to racial tensions in my high school, MU's predominately white leadership was surprised by and ill-equipped to respond to the emotions and context of the students' responses. In the fallout, members of the administration and faculty were confused. To them, Brown's death occurred in Ferguson, not on the campus of MU, and they couldn't grasp how one was so deeply connected to the other. Ferguson, Kansas City, St. Louis, and Chicago were where many of our Black students came from. What happened to Brown in Ferguson was their reality, and the administration couldn't grasp that fact—a fact that would require them to also acknowledge that systemic racism was present at MU.

The inaction of MU's leadership fueled tension, divisiveness, and, for the students of color, isolation. A quiet blanketed the campus as distance and distrust grew between students and faculty who didn't know what to say or how to say it. We began to receive reports from faculty that there was decreased dialogue in classrooms and growing pockets of students who just weren't showing up. I could feel and understand the outrage and pain of the students of color. They had no representation in senior leadership and very little representation across the whole of the administration and faculty—they felt alone in this fight.

It all came to a head in the fall of 2015.

In September of 2015, MU's student body president, Payton Head, who is Black, reported being called racial slurs by passengers in a pickup truck while walking on campus.[1] This incident was followed by additional reports of racist graffiti and harassment, including a

---

1 "The incidents that led to the University of Missouri president's resignation," *The Washington Post*, November 9, 2015, https://www.washingtonpost.com/news/grade-point/wp/2015/11/09/the-incidents-that-led-to-the-university-of-missouri-presidents-resignation/.

swastika drawn in human feces found in a residence hall bathroom in October.[2]

In response to these incidents and what students felt were insufficient responses from then–system president Tim Wolfe and campus chancellor R. Bowen Loftin regarding on-campus issues of racial discrimination, student activist group Concerned Student 1950 (1950 is the year that MU was ordered by the courts to enroll Black students) was formed.

The group began organizing protests and demanding action from the university administration. Concerned Student 1950 also presented a list of demands to university leadership, including the removal of President Tim Wolfe, increased hiring of Black faculty and staff, a mandatory racial awareness and inclusion curriculum, and increased funding for mental health professionals and social workers of color.[3]

Still, Wolfe and Loftin failed to directly engage with their concerns, which led to a pivotal protest staged during MU's homecoming parade on October 10, 2015. In the weeks that followed, the administration would once again host town halls to address student concerns related to the racial climate on campus, and students continued to push back that no progress was being made to address the issues.

On November 2, 2015, at nine in the morning, Jonathan L. Butler, one of the founders of Concerned Student 1950, began a hunger strike, calling for Wolfe's resignation.

---

2 "UPDATE: Swastika drawn with human feces found in MU residence hall," *Columbia Missourian*, October 29, 2015, https://www.columbiamissourian.com/news/higher_education/update-swastika-drawn-with-human-feces-found-in-mu-residence-hall/article_4f9c57f0-7f4c-11e5-9f88-a324bf705d1d.html.

3 "Concerned Student 1950 reissues list of demands," *KRCGTV*, February 24, 2016, https://krcgtv.com/news/local/concerned-student-1950-reissues-list-of-demands.

> *Let it be known I have no ill will or thoughts of harm towards Mr. Wolfe but I do have an urgency to make the campus I call home a more safe, welcoming, and inclusive environment for all identities and backgrounds. I am a firm believer that attending to the needs of marginalized/underrepresented students is worth the time, attention, and care of our administration; our lived experiences are worth acknowledging and our humanity worth fighting for. Starting today November 2, 2015 at 9:00 a.m. I will be embarking on an indefinite hunger strike ... until either Tim Wolfe is removed from office or my internal organs fail and my life is lost.*[4]

During Jonathan's hunger strike, I went to the encampment that housed him and his supporters to offer my support. I didn't visit the students simply as an administrator; these students were my students. Jonathan had been one of my graduate assistants the year before, and about half of the undergrads who made up Concerned Student 1950 had worked for me at some point during their undergraduate career. These brave young men and women were very much my students.

I will tell you that when I stepped into that space, I was in awe of what these students had created. Where I had expected sadness and despair, I found rich engagement between the core protestors who were staying close to Jonathan, visitors, and those coordinating the protest actions occurring beyond the boundaries of the encampment. There was soft music, food, and conversations that included strategy sessions, interspersed with lighthearted chatter and laughter. Most of all, there

---

4 Kasia Kovacs, "UPDATE: MU student embarks on hunger strike, demands Wolfe's removal from office," *Columbia Missourian*, November 2, 2015, https://www.columbiamissourian.com/news/higher_education/update-mu-student-embarks-on-hunger-strike-demands-wolfes-removal-from-office/article_35ab864a-8186-11e5-902b-6f136a45260b.html.

was commitment. Commitment to the mission, commitment to each other, and commitment to their fellow students. It was clear that Jonathan and his supporters would see what they had started through to its conclusion—no matter how drastic or severe.

I had come to support and lift their spirits, but if I'm honest, it was my spirit that was lifted. I was so inspired by and proud of all of them.

Jonathan's hunger strike became the focal point of the protest, and it drew significant media attention and increased the pressure on the administration to respond to student demands. On November 7, five days into Jonathan's hunger strike, the Missouri Tigers football team stepped up when approximately thirty Black players announced they would boycott all football activities until President Wolfe resigned. Their head coach and the entire coaching staff released a statement expressing solidarity with their players. The boycott increased media attention and support for Wolfe's resignation. It also created significant and immediate financial implications for the university, as it would be forced to cancel scheduled games.

On November 9, 2015, Wolfe resigned as president of the MU system. Wolfe's resignation would be followed by the resignation of University Chancellor Loftin several hours later.

In between those resignations, a statement was issued from the encampment that Jonathan was ending his hunger strike. To see Jonathan emerging from his tent so physically weak and wrapped in a blanket was surreal. But his focus was not on his health and well-being. His focus remained on the mission. He told the media to stop focusing on the hunger strike itself and instead look at why they had to struggle and fight so hard for change to happen.

"It should not have taken this much," he said. "And it is disgusting and vile that we find ourselves in a place that we do."[5]

Jonathan also made clear that this was not over. More change needed to come. To me, the most impactful change would be securing diversity in leadership and faculty. Students of color at MU were still without representative voices around decision-making. I was one of the few in those seats, and I wasn't even at the vice provost level. I was an assistant vice provost—but I was invited into that strategy session in the provost's office with cabinet- and vice provost–level leadership. There was a meeting, or rather a conversation between Dr. Spain and me after the meeting, that I want to return to for a moment.

It was as Jim and I walked back to our offices that the realization that I had been the only Black person in that strategy session on race hit me. How that realization might sit with me was not lost on Dr. Spain.

"Dr. Burns-Wallace," he began, "I don't want you to feel like we brought you into the room because we simply needed a Black person." He paused. "While we clearly did need a Black person's perspective, I suggested we bring you in because I knew you could bring the rich informed expertise and perspective this moment required."

I appreciated Jim's acknowledgment that there had been many meetings over these past several months when administration pulled those of us of color into meetings simply because we were of color and they felt compelled to fill that void with a face rather than a voice. I had been pulled into some of those meetings. That was not Dr. Spain's way. He modeled for other leaders on campus how to intentionally and continuously ensure that all necessary perspectives were seated

5 Eli Stokols, "Jonathan Butler: How a grad student's hunger strike toppled a university president," *NBC News*, November 9, 2015, https://www.nbcnews.com/news/us-news/jonathan-butler-how-grad-students-hunger-strike-toppled-university-president-n460161.

around strategy and decision-making tables and the importance of holding leaders accountable when that wasn't happening.

I highlight these students and their fight against systemic racial discrimination and disparities as I transitioned from MU to KU because everything they were fighting for was needed. KU was proof of that. While there were individuals in leadership roles at MU such as Dr. Spain, the fact remains that a diversity champion who does not look like or share the lived experiences of the underrepresented is not enough.

KU was certainly not immune to student protests or students who pushed the administration and demanded change, but the institution was better positioned to navigate those circumstances because it had the diversity of leadership in place. Chancellor Gray-Little served in that capacity from 2009 to 2017. She was the first and only woman and the first and only African American to serve in that role since the school's inception in 1867.

The members of Chancellor Gray-Little's Council of Deans, as well as members of her senior leadership, included women and people of color. My transition from MU to KU in that period made it abundantly clear to me that, without true diversity of voices at the leadership table, your organization is not equipped to deal with issues of race, equity, belonging, inclusion, and even responsiveness. It is really that simple.

CHAPTER 19
FEELING GOOD

"Feeling Good"

It's a new day
It's a new life for me, ooh
And I'm feeling good

—Nina Simone

The combined support, knowledge, and experience I had gained through my time at Stanford, my ACE fellowship, and MU culminated in a sense of preparedness and confidence for my new position as vice provost for undergraduate education more than any previous role. But the other change my new position necessitated—yet another move—did not inspire the same sense of assuredness in me.

X and I had spent most of his life going back and forth. One of his primary memories of our time in Columbia is going back and forth between home and his G and G-Pa (my parents), his dad, and his nana (his dad's mom) in Kansas City. While he had spent significant time with them in those early years, they were always *there*, and we were always *here*. As I contemplated buying a house and establishing honest-to-goodness roots for the two of us, I would come to realize that it was not as simple as finding a house near campus and moving into it.

To begin with, X and I would need in-between housing while I figured this out. As you may have guessed, we once again moved into my parents' basement for what I promised myself would be the last time.

KU is in Lawrence, Kansas, and my parents' home is on the Missouri side of Kansas City, which meant, with traffic, I was spending at least two hours a day commuting. So when I first began my house search, I was focused on the area in and around Lawrence. As that process evolved, my parents and I began having the conversation about how they could continue to support me and X when I wasn't able to pick him up for school or take him to soccer, or when I was traveling—all those usual things.

During this period, my father was also preparing to retire, and my parents were thinking of downsizing. They were both still young, in their early sixties, with busy, active lives connected to Kansas City. My parents having to drive an hour or more each way wasn't feasible either. It was never our intention to continue to live in the same house, but as we talked more about it, it just made sense.

I found a house in a suburb of Kansas City, on the Kansas side, that was close enough for my parents to get to their church and doctors and visit with family and friends and was a reasonable commute for me. Now, if anyone had told me I would buy a house with a basement that my parents would move into *and* we would all still be living together nine-plus years later, I would have said, "No, that would be crazy." I mean, my parents were still so young and active, and I was now able to financially afford a home of my own, so at no time did my parents or I say, "Let's all live together!" But through the ebbs and flows, we've found our rhythm over the years and have made it work for all of us.

And that was no truer than when the world stopped in 2020. During COVID-19, I had so many friends who had stories about worrying about their parents and trying to figure out how they could safely see them. They sometimes had to quickly create ad hoc quarantine houses and throw their lives together. When the world shut down, my parents, X, and I were already where we needed to be. By then, my dad was already on in-home dialysis. I truly believe everything happens for a reason, and there is a time and a season for all of it.

It was July 1, 2016, when I officially became a homeowner for the first time. I can still remember feeling anxious, overwhelmed, and so excited when I picked up the key that afternoon. When I returned to my parents' home, there were boxes everywhere—all of them ready to go to my new home. As I stood in what had been my childhood bedroom, assessing what still needed to be packed, I heard the doorbell ring and then my mother call up to me, "There's somebody here to see you, DeAngela."

I walked down the hall and peered over the railing to the living room below. My mother and father were standing there, and next to them was one of my best friends from college, Alison. I stared at the three of them for a long moment, "Alison?" I finally said. "What are you doing here?"

"Didn't you get the keys to your new house today?" she asked.

"Yeah," I said slowly, still not fully registering that she was standing in our living room.

"Well, I rented a truck. We're moving, right?"

To this day, the four of us still laugh about that moment. Honestly, I shouldn't have been surprised Alison was there—should have expected it. Alison, by the way, lives in Atlanta, Georgia—nowhere near Kansas City. But Alison is family. My parents think of her as a daughter, and she thinks of them as parents. Alison's parents and I feel the same way.

When Kelly and I made the transition to California for my new position at Stanford in 2004, Alison's parents stepped in and took care of us. They lived in the Bay Area, and Kelly and I lived in their basement (I didn't realize until I wrote this book how frequently basements came to my rescue) for a few months while we searched for a place of our own. Alison was my maid of honor when I married Kelly, and a month later, I was her matron of honor as she married her soul mate, Alpha. It was my mother who did Alison's hair the morning of her wedding. Like I said, I should not have been surprised when she arrived, ready to help.

As Alison was hauling boxes and bags of my dad's clothes into the truck that day, she said to my dad, "I don't know that I have ever known any man who has more clothes than you, Daddy Burns. And," she added, "they're heavy as hell."

Alison and I drove the first load over, but before we brought anything in, I gave her a tour of my new home. And then, she and I sat in my empty living room and talked about where we both were in life and how we got there. More accurately, I should say that Alison pushed me to reflect on my journey that led me back home. "So," she began, "you didn't want to come home. But have you reflected on how that has really transformed your journey?" I said nothing because I knew what was coming next, and I didn't want to have to tell her she was right until I absolutely had to. "And," she continued, "that it was the best thing for you?" Alison is a deep thinker and pushes you to answer questions like *How do you feel about this?* or *Have you stopped to think about what this means?* Those types of reflections are in me, but because of how I compartmentalize, I don't always address them. Alison, of course, knows this, but she never lets me off the hook, and I'm forced to admit that the opportunities in front of me at KU and in building a home for X, my parents, and me so close to family and friends are absolutely the right ones.

That time with Alison is my first memory of my new home—a memory that serves as the foundation of so many wonderful memories that followed.

After a few weeks of moving trucks, movers, trips to storage units, and the unpacking of boxes, the four of us officially moved in, and the construction of my parents' own space in the basement began. The basement was completely unfinished—which turned out to be a huge plus because my mom was able to channel her interior design talent and skills to create their own space exactly as she wanted it. I remember the builder letting her know what cabinets and molding and whatever it was he was going to use and her replying, "No, no. I will identify what materials and products you install in my home." End of discussion. My parents were able to move into their home within my home before Christmas that same year. The following spring, our multigenerational living arrangement would inspire my friend, Jason Glenn (JG), to move his mom from Los Angeles to Kansas City to live with him as well.

JG and I were undergrads together at Stanford. We both attended the fellowship dinner in our sophomore year. We didn't really know each other at that time, but by our senior year, we would serve together as resident assistants in our African American–themed dorm at Stanford, Ujamaa. That experience created a lifelong friendship. I had been with KU for about a year and a half when I got a call from

JG, who said, "Hey, Dee, I'm coming to Kansas City to interview for a job at the University of Kansas."

JG would be offered and accept the position and move to Kansas City. My home served as his in-between housing for the first couple of months while he found his own place. And it was during that time with us that he was inspired to move his mom from Los Angeles to Kansas City to live with him.

As participants in that sophomore fellowship dinner so many years ago, JG and I both shared a passion for improving student success and expanding access to students of color, just as Stanford had done for us. While our roles at KU were separate and distinct, that shared passion would unite us in a full circle moment just months after he arrived.

CHAPTER 20
LEAN ON ME

"Lean on Me"

When you're not strong
And I'll be your friend
I'll help you carry on

—Bill Withers

elcome to KU's first annual Rising Scholars Brunch!"

Looking out over the expansive room filled with nearly two hundred sophomores seated at tables adorned with elegant linens, beautiful floral arrangements, and colorful balloon bouquets, and with "Welcome Scholars" banners lining the walls, I felt the profound significance of this full circle moment on so many levels.

If you recall, the fellowship dinner that led to my Pickering Fellowship was made possible by the head of Stanford's Office of

Undergraduate Research, who intentionally crafted an event for sophomores of color with a high GPA to come together with faculty and upper-class students for the purpose of connecting and nurturing fellowship opportunities. I now fully understood the power that opportunity provided to me, and I was committed to replicating it for the students of KU.

In 2018, my team and I were proud to host KU's first annual Rising Scholars Brunch.

We had invited almost two hundred sophomores to this early Saturday morning event in April. The students had no idea what this event was or even how they were identified. Whether they would show up was our biggest fear. They did! The event was designed to celebrate sophomore scholars from various backgrounds, including first-generation students, low-income students, and students of color, and introduce them to and guide them through the world of fellowships.

Over brunch, they met a cohort of their sophomore peers. They connected with faculty, many of whom reflected their diversity and identities and served as mentors—mentors these students didn't know they had access to. And finally, they were introduced to upper-class students—upper-class students they could see themselves in and who made them believe that they, too, could reach the same heights. I am proud to say that as of the writing of this book, this event is in its seventh year and counting.

Our second annual Rising Scholars Brunch in 2019 was another full circle moment for me. To be the keynote speaker at the second annual event and to look out and see JG, a friend who started this journey with me, as we introduced the next generation to all their possibilities was a moment filled with so many emotions. To know that one of the faculty members, this amazing African American man from Los Angeles, would inspire these students to dream big and to know that the two of us had sat in these seats while our role models inspired and taught us to dream big felt so incredible, so humbling, and so right. We were both exactly where we were supposed to be.

To watch these beautiful students carry the energy and hope created in that room out into that bright Saturday morning with them—the same energy and hope that so many individuals had helped JG and me create and carry forward—was a gift beyond measure. "You did this, Dee," JG said to me as we walked down the steps of the Kansas Memorial Union. So many thoughts swirled in my mind. Yes, our passions often lead us to the work we do and the roles and capacities in which we serve, but passion alone is not enough. As leaders, we must also embrace a deep appreciation for our role in carrying that work forward. The Pickering Fellowship had been my pathway to all I wanted to accomplish, and my work is reflective of my understanding of how key the opportunity to connect with a fellowship was and how that connection happened because of intentional, systemic change made by the Ambassador Davises, Secretary Powells, Anna Marie Porrases, and Chancellor Gray-Littles before me.

But in this moment, my most prominent thought was appreciation for my friend beside me. JG, too, shared this deep appreciation. He, too, understood the pivotal role he played as a Black male university faculty member in lifting the next generation of young leaders. We could both see what the Mama Jewels and Jeanette Smith-Laws saw in us and did for us so many years ago.

In moments like these, I know the work is still necessary, but I also know that I don't have to worry whether the work will continue because there are so many who carry that mantle alongside me—people like JG and the other mentors in that room. I also know that some of the students in that very room would one day be ready to step up and carry that mantle in the future. I was honored to help them prepare for that moment, just as I had been honored to prepare my team of recruiters during my time in admission at Stanford to do similar work.

My time at Stanford was spent cultivating, coaching, and encouraging a team of recruiters who represented the diverse student populations we were seeking to engage. We would have deep and thoughtful dialogues about how to shape the next diverse class of freshmen. These conversations were based on data and each recruiter's own expertise about their community. While I was out on maternity leave, they held one of these sessions on their own. In that session, they all wore T-shirts that read, "What would DBW do?" When they first told me this, I thought, *Y'all are crazy!* But I was also incredibly humbled to see that, just as I still often asked myself, *What would Anna Marie do? What would Ambassador Davis do? What would Mama Jewel do?*, I now serve as that reflection point for those coming up behind me. This is why I do the work that I do.

There was yet another full circle moment for me at KU. That moment came through the power of introducing undergraduate research opportunities to a group of students who are often overlooked for such opportunities. It was a mirror image of my journey.

While my own sophomore fellowship dinner opened me to the world of fellowships, it also provided me with access to undergraduate research opportunities. It was at that fellowship dinner that I met world-renowned historian Dr. Kennell Jackson Jr., who would serve as my honors thesis advisor and with whom I would forge a deep, long-lasting relationship. That access and opportunity to research would propel my senior honors thesis, which in turn would provide me with the opportunity to graduate with honors from Stanford University.

To have a professor like Dr. Jackson, who looked like me and who so graciously made a call that would grant me access to TransAfrica—a research, education, and advocacy center dedicated to global justice for the African world—had a profound impact on my confidence and understanding of how to research in an intimate and powerful way and to not shy away from or feel the need to water down topics associated with race.

During the summer I spent in DC at TransAfrica in 1995, I wasn't dusting off history books for my research. I was embedded in an institution and its people who had played an important role in dismantling apartheid in South Africa—a role that had led to the election of Nelson Mandela, South Africa's first Black president, in 1994. To be granted such access was a true gift. A gift that helped me understand the level of excellence that results from the purity and strength of such intimate and honest research. A gift that I would intentionally pay forward at every opportunity.

During my role at KU was one of many times I paid it forward. At KU, the undergraduate research department fell under my purview. This unit focused its resources on the upper-class students with high GPAs in their majors. It worked to ensure that those students with the strongest academic profiles had additional opportunities to conduct research with faculty. This department traditionally sought out upper-class students with high GPAs, matched them with faculty members, and then helped them obtain research dollars and do presentations because these students were deemed the best and the brightest. If you didn't meet those finite standards, you weren't invited into the program.

Stanford did not put limiting parameters around who could do research. If you wanted to do undergraduate research, you went to the undergraduate research office and were given the tools and opportunities to do so. The people at that office didn't care what your GPA was because they understood that intellectual curiosity was not measured in a GPA. It was a research institute, and the faculty was excited when students wanted to explore a path of research. I wanted to see this opportunity open to all interested students at KU. We began strategizing change by asking the team at the KU office of undergraduate research a few questions: Who would they like to serve? Who weren't they serving, and why? Which students were not taking advantage of undergraduate research, and did we understand why not?

We found that the students who came from lower-income backgrounds weren't being served because undergraduate research didn't typically pay, and the time commitment research internships required made it impossible to also maintain a job. Additionally, undergraduate research students incurred costs associated with their research work, such as attending conferences, presenting, and printing materials. And again, this office also traditionally only focused on juniors and seniors for these opportunities, based on the assumption that freshmen and sophomores were not quite ready to engage at this level.

At Stanford, I never had to think about whether I could afford to do undergrad research because Stanford's Office of Undergraduate Research provided research grants to cover all my research-related expenses. I struggled enough to pay my tuition bill; it would have been impossible for me to also cover my research expenses. I would have been one of those passed-over students.

The critical components of my vision for KU undergraduate studies were shaped by my work at MU and Stanford. One key piece of that success was my colleague, trusted advisor, and friend, Susan Klusmeier. Susan joined me at KU six months after I left MU. She knew the work and had been a tremendous partner as my number two at MU. She also had KU ties, as she had completed her master's degree there. Susan was an integral part of my strategy and our success in the work at both institutions. There was a bonus: Susan's in-laws were living in Kansas City, giving me an opportunity to bring my friend and her family home.

In true *Grey's Anatomy* fashion, Susan is Christina to my Meredith. Back in my role as assistant vice provost at MU, I would send open invitations for anyone to come and talk with me. One day, Susan took me up on my invitation. The first time we met, Susan shared that the work she was doing just wasn't what she needed it to be, and she was very excited about some of the work my office was doing around access and student success. Initially, our relationship was more of a professional mentorship. I'd help her talk through how she could navigate what she was facing in her work. A few months later, when I needed to expand my shop at MU and hire an assistant director, I immediately thought of Susan. That would begin our journey of a partnership and friendship—a circle of support—that now spans more than ten years.

Susan is brilliant and meticulous. She's me on steroids in terms of details. When I throw a big vision up in the air, she always figures out how to execute it. "Well," she always begins, "if we do that, we need to do this and this and that." And then together, we make it happen. For me, it is a beautiful thing because, even though many of my teams get excited and empowered by the visions and innovations that I bring and how I push and how fast I push, very few can keep up. And that's challenging for me when implementing new concepts, policies, or programming.

I shared with Susan my vision for a new program for work-study students to be able to do undergraduate research as freshmen and sophomores and to use their work-study dollars to make that happen. It had the potential to be a game changer for freshmen and sophomores coming from lower-income backgrounds to gain access to a faculty member and to the dollars and support to do research.

When I shared it with the office that would oversee this program, I received substantial pushback: "They're freshmen and sophomores, and they're coming from a lower-income background. These students aren't prepared. They can't do this." But Susan understood where we were going and how to get us there. Susan became the DBW "translator" when the directors under me would come to her and say, "We like the idea, but we don't understand what DeAngela wants us to do or how we are supposed to execute it."

Susan was instrumental in helping them clarify the what and how, and as we overlaid this new perspective and focus, we created an Emerging Scholars Program that opened undergrad research to freshmen and sophomores who were federal work-study students. Their federal work-study dollars paid for 75 percent of their research salary, and the other 25 percent would come from a grant out of my office. Those research students were available at no cost to the research faculty. Removing those barriers opened new opportunities for a group of students typically overlooked in undergraduate research.

We went on to break down more barriers and open more pathways and opportunities across our student body, from helping students clear financial balances so that they could enroll to expanding summer preparation and orientation opportunities for our underrepresented minority students to help them get a jump start on their transition.

Opening access to fellowships and undergraduate research opportunities was powerful and represented full circle moments. So many had opened doors for me, and every door that I helped to open for others fueled my purpose and passion for my life's work.

I love the vision that Ralph Waldo Emerson's quote, "The mind, once stretched by a new idea, never returns to its original dimensions," evokes. I've come to learn and embrace that when you intentionally infuse new ideas, new concepts, and new structural ways of doing things, people may not agree 100 percent, and they may not do everything you want them to do, but they can't unknow it. If you put the pieces together well, they begin to move differently, they begin to build differently, and they begin to structure themselves differently. The intentional change of how we thought about student success was the true power of the work I led at KU.

By the spring of 2019, we had just finished a strategic plan that my entire division had participated in. The right leadership team was in place, and we all understood the mission, what we intended to accomplish, and how to fulfill our mission in different and systemic ways. We were firing on all cylinders. And then, the governor's office called.

CHAPTER 21

GIRL ON FIRE

“Girl on Fire”

She got her head in the clouds and she’s not backin’ down
THIS GIRL IS ON FIRE

—Alicia Keys

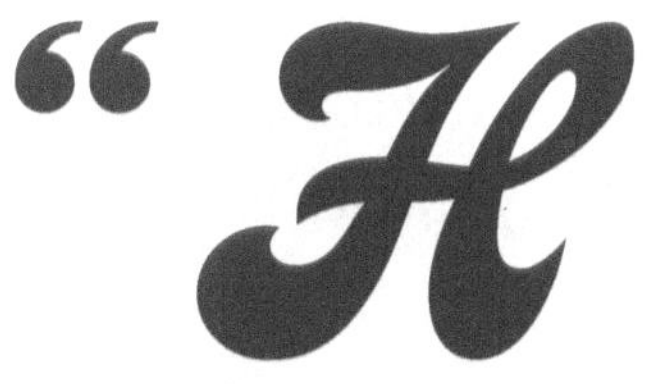

ello, Dr. Burns-Wallace. My name is Scott, and I’m the director of appointments with Governor Kelly’s office. We’d like to talk to you about an opportunity …”

That was the voice message I retrieved shortly after I concluded my presentation on student success, data analytics, and predictive modeling at the annual South by Southwest Education (SXSW EDU) Conference in March of 2019. SXSW EDU is said to bring together the brightest minds in education to share ideas, network, and create the future of teaching and learning. To be on the main stage at SXSW EDU was truly a bucket list item that I could not believe I was checking off.

As I searched for a quiet space to replay the message from the governor's office, I ran into my friend Jenny—we had received our doctorates together—and we huddled in the hall to listen to the message. "We'd like to talk to you about an opportunity ..." the message said as I replayed it for Jenny. I can still see us standing near a window and giggling like two schoolgirls as we took turns blurting out ideas of what the governor might ask me to do. We thought a commission on higher education or a senior role shaping higher education policy for the state was among the top possibilities. Boy, were we wrong!

In late March 2019, I drove down I-70 from Lawrence to Topeka and pulled into the underground parking garage at the Kansas State Capitol building. As I walked into the meeting, still in the dark about what I was going to be asked to do, my curiosity kicked into high gear. The director of appointments and the chief of staff introduced themselves, and over the next thirty minutes, I shared my background, interests, and more. As I completed my intro and mini presentation of my qualifications, the chief of staff leaned forward and said, "We've done our background research on you, we've obtained references, and Governor Kelly would like you to consider being her secretary of administration."

Anyone who knows me knows that in a moment like this, I do not have a poker face. In these moments, my face will tell you exactly what I'm thinking, and, as you can imagine, I was thinking about a lot. I knew I only had a few moments before my face would reveal everything, from utter surprise to total disbelief. I told myself, *DeAngela, wrap this meeting up and get out of this office ASAP.* I pulled myself together, asked a few questions about the timeline and process, requested they send me a few pieces of information, and then headed for the door. I am not sure I heard any of their answers that day, but I smiled and did my best to appear composed.

Once I was back in my car, I could just imagine how my quickly changing emotions were playing on my face. The furrow of my brow (*is this really happening?*), the lighting up of my eyes (*oh my God, this is really happening*), the fall of my face (*how can I leave my team at KU?*), and on and on as thoughts raced through my mind. I took a deep breath and began to process more slowly. My work at KU was not done. We had so much more potential, and I wanted to keep us moving. Could I pause my position at KU, take the job with the governor, and then come back and finish the work that still needed to be done at KU?

At the same time, I recognized and was excited by the opportunity that had been put before me. The governor's team sought me out because they thought I was a match for what she needed to accomplish her vision—but I still didn't feel ready to leave KU. I continued my internal debate until, in a moment, I thought, *How arrogant are you, DeAngela, to think the leadership team you built can't continue to do this work without you?* I recognized that I needed to move my ego out of the way and give every person on that team their due credit for the power of who they were and what they had achieved and would continue to accomplish.

If, in this moment, I could not move my ego out of the way, then my belief that true social and systemic change cannot happen if the work and impact are tied only to the individual leader would be a lie. And all my talk about how *we can do this together* and *it's not about me* would also be a lie.

I knew my belief and my words were not a lie. I knew that my team at KU was fully capable of continuing their impactful work with or without me at the helm.

When I returned to the Capitol the first week of April to meet with the governor, I had made my decision to accept the position of secretary of administration. I had done my homework in weighing the pros and cons of this significant decision. I had done my research on Governor Laura Kelly and the role she was asking me to fill. I had met with members of her team, including the sitting secretary. I had drawn on the wisdom of trusted mentors. And I had worked through the necessary shift in my commute—I was not moving my family—and what it would mean for my son and my parents.

People ask me about the weight of the moment when I walked into the Capitol to meet with Governor Kelly and accept the position of secretary of administration. My response is not what most people expect. I was not full of nerves or doubt. No what-if scenarios were circling in my brain. What I unequivocally felt was excitement for the opportunity before me and an eagerness to get started, just as I had the first time I drove onto Stanford's campus as a freshman and the first time I entered the US Department of State in DC as a candidate for the Pickering Fellowship. Sometimes, you just know that you are exactly where you are meant to be. And when I know, when I have made my decision, I'm full steam ahead. So, as I entered the Kansas State Capitol that day, I was excited to meet the governor and eager to tell her I was ready to go. But first, I would have to get to her.

Walking the path to the governor's inner sanctum is like navigating a labyrinth because it's not just one room; it's an entire sequence of spaces that begins with the outer ceremonial office, a grand and inspiring space steeped in history and ceremony. At its center sits the beautiful handcrafted walnut ceremonial desk, which I would later learn was made by students at the Kansas School for the Deaf in Olathe during the 1930s. From there, I was ushered around a corner and through another door that opened to a long, hallway-like room lined with immense windows, which housed the governor's assistant and other support staff members.

I took in everything I could about the spaces I was walking through, partially because of my training as an FSO and partly because of my own curiosity. But as I walked through these incredible spaces, I tried to grasp the dynamic and the structure of the offices. *Who were all these people I had yet to meet? Would I meet them all and work with them all? Were these spaces that I would frequent?* These were the questions running through my mind, followed by, *Am I ever going to reach the governor's office?*

At the very end of that long room, there was yet another door. Once I crossed that threshold, I was finally in the governor's inner office space.

I was in awe, yes, as I joined Governor Kelly at the conference table in the small space adjoining the governor's actual office, but I also felt at ease in this intimate space to which I was invited. While it is no secret that Governor Kelly is a confident, clear, and directive leader, she was also personable, instantly making connections by mentioning my alma mater, UPenn, where her daughter was also an alum, and the people we had in common. Once we got to know each other a bit, her director of appointments, Scott, and her chief of staff, Will, joined us. That is when Governor Kelly, framed by the large, beautiful picture window behind her, leaned forward, looked me square in the eye, and said, "So are we going to do this or what?"

I would come to understand that this was Governor Laura Kelly in her truest form—no nonsense, let's get it done. We talked in more detail about the position and process, and later that week, I would accept the position, which would kick into motion background checks, announcement plans, and all the other components of the process. My new position would be announced in the first week of June, and I would move into my role as secretary of administration for the state of Kansas on July 1, 2019.

When I got home that evening, my dad was sitting at the kitchen counter, watching TV. I looked at him and said very matter-of-factly, "So, Governor Kelly wants me to come be her secretary of administration." The two of us just sat there, staring at each other for a few moments. I think it was because neither of us really knew what that meant.

Once it sunk in, my dad said, "I'm so proud of you."

My conversation with my mom a few minutes later was very different. "How much are you going to get paid?" was my mom's first question, followed by, "Are you planning to move down there?" I just had to laugh. How my parents react to big news has always been like night and day. My mom, always thinking tactically, and my dad, always responding with the emotional aspect of the moment. It's a good balance.

"If you're happy, Mom, I'm happy," was my son's response when I told him that I might be leaving KU for a new big job. By the time my position was officially announced, X understood that I would be holding an important position within the state—although at nine years old, my level of importance was relative. The day the governor made the official announcement, X and my parents were there, and X kept telling everyone, "My mommy runs the state."

"No, baby," I would explain. "Governor Kelly runs the state, and I am part of the team that helps her do that." But he had already made up his mind that I was in charge.

Long before that official announcement was made, still in awe about the opportunity I was about to embark upon, I wondered how I had landed there. How had my name entered the governor's vision of what her cabinet and administration would look like? So, when I had the chance to ask Governor Kelly, I did.

It was during the period when we were working through all the details of my departure from KU and entrance to the state that I asked, "How did you find me?"

Governor Kelly explained that when she was building her cabinet, she tapped into her trusted advisors, letting them know that she was building a team of the best transformational leaders. It didn't matter what their party or background was; what mattered was that they knew how to lead and how to get work done. (My direct support staff quickly learned I was a leader who got stuff done when they found me, an hour into my first day as secretary of administration, crawling under my desk so I could connect cables—too impatient to wait for IT. I can still hear one of my lead IT team members, Charlene, exclaiming, "Oh my God, Secretary, get off the floor!") Although my name had popped up through a few different channels, she told me that it was Reggie Robinson who really brought my name to her attention.

I smiled, thinking of a day back at KU when Reggie, vice chancellor for public affairs and one of my KU colleagues, had hurriedly come into a meeting in the chancellor's conference room. Several of us were seated around the table, and as Reggie sat down, he said to me, "Your ears should be ringing, Dr. Burns-Wallace. Your name is being spoken in hallways in Topeka."

I can remember thinking that somebody else could go fight with Topeka to get our money. If I had to go down there and testify, so be it, but I wasn't playing in Topeka; that was Reggie's arena. And on we went with the meeting. I hadn't thought anything of it until that moment.

After my conversation with the governor, I went to see Reggie. Standing in the doorway to his office, I laughed and asked, "Why would you do this?"

As we both took a seat on his sofa beneath the window overlooking The Hill and the Memorial Campanile, he said with complete confidence, "I couldn't think of anyone better. DeAngela, you have everything Governor Kelly needs." In my first year as secretary of administration, Reggie would be a trusted mentor I would frequently call upon for advice. When the governor asked me to take on the second secretarial seat in the role of chief information officer, I called Reggie and asked, "Am I crazy if I take this?" At every turn, Reggie would say to me, "Trust what you know; trust what you've already done. I have no doubts about what you can do."

Reggie was a true thought partner and champion as I joined the leadership team at KU. I enjoyed and learned so much from the many deep philosophical debates about life and politics that I had with this beautiful African American man, whose smile and deep, wonderful laugh welcomed and inspired everyone who crossed his path. We would lose Reggie to cancer the following year, on September 19, 2020.

A few years later, when I was honored by the governor during Women's History Month in 2023, Reggie's youngest daughter, Paige, whom I had the good fortune of getting to know well when she began working in the governor's office, introduced me to her mom, Jane Robinson. As we hugged deeply, she whispered in my ear, "Reggie would be so proud of you." That meant the world to me.

Reggie had, unbeknownst to me, carried my name into a room because of what he saw in me and the confidence he had in me. He never told me what he had done. He had only said in passing, "Your ears should be ringing, Dr. Burns-Wallace." That's the leader I try to be.

At every turn, I look to see whom I can carry into the room—whom I can create an opportunity for. I want to carry Reggie's legacy of lifting and leading into the future. I want to serve as the catalyst for opportunity for all individuals who are growing, trying, and striving toward their full potential, but particularly for women and, most especially, for women of color.

The in-between weeks from when I accepted the position to when it was announced were incredibly challenging for many reasons. But the biggest reason was not being able to share my news with anyone outside of my immediate family. No one else could know until after the state had completed its intensive vetting process and presented me to its senate leadership.

Working alongside my team at KU while knowing I was leaving but unable to share that with them was incredibly difficult. In the weeks that followed, every action I took at KU was with the understanding and preparation that I would not be there by July 1, and I did my best to set my team and the institution up for a successful transition. I had just spent the last three and a half years putting into place everything that led us to this moment of tremendous opportunity for systemic change, and to not be able to see it through alongside my amazing team was tough. I had already envisioned how what we were on the brink of implementing would be humming like a beautiful machine in two or three years and how the resulting outcomes would position me to potentially move to a university presidency. So, as excited and as honored as I was to be chosen, this was bittersweet in so many ways.

By May, I had passed my background checks and had been presented to senate leadership with no objections. We knew we were moving forward now, and I had about three weeks before the announcement came out to share the news with key people. So, of course, it was Susan whom I told first because she would be the person most impacted by my departure. The chancellor at the time was my mentor and friend, Chancellor Douglas A. Girod. It was during these three weeks that he and I were able to finally have the conversation about my new role. I was incredibly thankful for Doug's full support throughout this transition, his recognition of the importance of how impactful my work could be at that next state level, and his belief in continuing the work I started while at KU.

One week prior to the announcement, I was given the green light to share with my leadership team at KU, but no one else. Who is informed about these political appointments—and how—is highly orchestrated to avoid them being derailed before they even get started. I was thankful I could tell my immediate team in advance, as I didn't want them to find out along with the public. On June 1, the governor's announcement would go out, followed by the KU chancellor's announcement regarding my departure and congratulations on my new role with the state.

Sharing the news with my team was hard. But I knew, and the team members knew, that they were prepared for the work. Susan would take the reins, initially serving as interim vice provost of undergraduate education and then moving into the role permanently. While it was hard to tell my team I was leaving, it wasn't hard to explain my why. As employees of a state institution, we saw ourselves as serving the state and the citizens of our state for their betterment. So, while people were sad and disappointed, there were many moments of excitement and appreciation for what I could do for the state of Kansas and its citizens in my new position.

My senate confirmation hearings were held in July 2019 as I started my new role with the state. It was a rigorous but relatively smooth process. There was a moment—in fact, one of the very last questions—when the depth of my experience was challenged by one of the senators. He suggested that my years of service with the State Department (my Foreign Service tenure) didn't add up to the total years of experience I said I had. I politely walked him back to my beginnings with the State Department as a Pickering fellow at the age of nineteen and the multiple domestic and international internship tours I experienced before beginning my official career as an FSO.

When the hearings had concluded, one of my colleagues in the governor's office said with a smile, "You made him do the math."

I did make him do the math because the depth of my experience is real. There is nothing padded in what I bring to the table, and I needed to make that clear. This was not the first time someone would suggest that I looked a little too good on paper to be true. Part of the fun of being far more prepared and qualified than people expect is seeing the looks on their faces when you surpass all their expectations of you, just like you knew you would and just like those who prepared you expected you to.

CHAPTER 22
ROAR

"Roar"

I got the eye of the tiger, a fighter
Dancing through the fire
'Cause I am a champion, and you're gonna hear me roar

—Katy Perry

For so long, you have been told to be invisible because you are administration, because you are the backdrop, because you're not seen, because you just make stuff work. But I need you all to know that what we are going to be is seamless and *visible. We will be visible because people need to know it does not work without us and without investing in us.* — *DeAngela Burns-Wallace, EdD*

lmost immediately after I came into the role of secretary of administration for the state of Kansas, I did a walk-around. Because the Department of Administration is such a complex organization,

I had ten direct reports who were physically all over Topeka. I met each of them and their teams at their locations. They would walk me around their facilities so that I could see the work they were doing, and then we would gather with their teams, which could be as small as fifteen and as large as a few hundred.

At these meetings, I shared a little bit about myself and what I hoped to do in my role in terms of learning, listening, and supporting them as we moved forward. I told the members of the department that I would rely on them to teach me about their operations because, of course, they knew them better than I did. It was in these settings that I would share my "We will be visible" speech. My focus on visibility was based on everything I had observed and heard. The Department of Administration staff was only made visible when there was a problem or when it was used as a scapegoat when another department didn't properly navigate an issue.

For example, if a particular agency didn't get its information in on time or didn't follow the proper procurement process and delayed a contract, it would be said, "Oh, the Department of Administration's procurement processes slowed us down." This narrative was so commonplace that, regardless of whether it was truly to blame, the Department of Administration would just take it or assume that it was at fault.

I made a commitment to each of the staff members that people would know and understand the critical nature of the work they did, which kept the delivery of services for the state government running—services that transformed communities and changed and saved lives. I committed to providing the resources and support they needed to make our delivery seamless because their work was valuable. I asked them why they chose to do the work they do and what they would like to see me do and not do in my role as secretary of administration. "Together," I told them, "our presence will be felt for what we are able to accomplish."

Early in my career, I focused on the organization and what the organization needed and how to get what I needed out of people to meet the organization's needs. By the time I worked for the state of Kansas, I had long figured out that it's the other way around. When you understand the people and when you take care of the people, the people will give the organization what it needs.

I had always cared about the people I worked with. Even as a teenager supervising people at Worlds of Fun, I would physically check in with the other teenagers who were stuck in the ticket booths all day to let them know they weren't forgotten. But people weren't the lens through which I led then. Now, they are. I learned I must come to know the people first, what they do, and *why* they do it. It is only then that a leader can help their people see themselves in the mission and vision of the organization.

The leader cannot do everything, nor can they impose everything that needs to be done. They must empower their people to join them on the journey.

Over time, the conversation of accountability began to shift. The Department of Administration was responsible for the oversight of all capitol facilities. Frank Burnam, deputy secretary of operations and director of facilities and property management, had been in his role for several years and was highly respected. Since I arrived, I had heard nothing but accolades about Frank and his team's commitment to the work. So, in meetings when the conversation was about a facility issue, it would frequently end with talk about how unresponsive the facilities team was. I would counter with, "That's Frank's team. They are always responsive. Has anyone advised Frank and his team about the issue?"

The answer would be, "Well, no."

"So," I would reply, "if Frank doesn't know y'all need help with something, how can he fix it for you?"

Over those initial months, I made my presence known everywhere, and I touted our accomplishments at every turn. Eventually, when the Department of Administration was blamed, legislators and others outside of my department would ask, "Have you spoken to Secretary Burns-Wallace? I'm sure she can take care of that."

We started to become known as solution finders.

Accountability works both ways, and when we were at fault for missteps, I took full responsibility, and then my team and I fixed it. But I refused to sit silently or accept blame for things that were not my team's fault. I wasn't aggressive and I wasn't rude, but I didn't back down. Just as I took full responsibility when we didn't get it right, *we* took full ownership when we did. In those moments, I would require that the department and the team members responsible for the win be recognized for their effectiveness. My team no longer witnessed only the individuals who would testify before the legislature and throw our department under the bus or the articles that showed us in a bad light. At every turn, they would hear praise for all the impactful and critical things they delivered.

My reputation as a credible and accountable leader grew, and along with that came acknowledgment for my team. By the time of my official swearing in seven months later, it was no secret what the Department of Administration did and how well we did it.

I want to be clear: The work being done by the Department of Administration was important and impactful well before me. Changing the narrative, amplifying the success stories, and ensuring that our work and our team were visible were what I brought to the table. For me, the beauty of leading the department was the force and the heart of the staff and leadership who were behind the department's success from the beginning.

CHAPTER 23
CELEBRATION

"Celebration"

There's a party going on right here
A celebration to last throughout the years
So bring your good times and your laughter too

—Kool & the Gang

On January 19, 2020, the Kansas City Chiefs won the Super Bowl for the first time in fifty years! My family and I are die-hard Chiefs fans, and the Chiefs' Super Bowl celebration parade was happening on the same day as my proposed swearing in ceremony—February 5, 2020. As I write this, I know how crazy this sounds, but I had to tell Governor Kelly's office that if my family members had to choose between the Chiefs' parade and my swearing in, they might not show up for my swearing in. Yes, I am exaggerating a bit, but if I had been completely honest, I would have told them that I wasn't sure I would show up myself. We really are die-hard fans.

Let me back up a moment. Although I had been appointed and confirmed by what is known as the interim session by the senate in July 2019 and I had been serving in my role as secretary of administration for the state of Kansas since then, because it is a senate-confirmed role, my full confirmation required a full senate vote, which the summer session could not provide. Therefore, my full official confirmation came in late January when the full Senate was back in session. My swearing in ceremony was then scheduled for February 5, 2020, along with the swearing in of the secretary of corrections and the superintendent of the Kansas Highway Patrol, both fellow cabinet members.

After a few adjustments, my swearing in ceremony was rescheduled to later in the month, on Monday, February 17, Presidents' Day (which would also become a future special date for my dad). Because I was the only cabinet member being sworn in on February 17, I was able to invite more guests to the ceremony than was the norm.

My team orchestrated the logistics of this day, from checking the list of all my guests and any special accommodations, such as my grandmother needing a wheelchair, to ensuring everyone parked in the right spots before being ushered up to the Kansas Statehouse. Once all twenty-five of my family members and friends were gathered with me in the hallway, we entered Governor Kelly's ceremonial office as one.

In the center of the room sat a large ceremonial desk and podium. The chief justice, who would swear me in, and Xavier and I were standing in front while my family and friends filled out the edges of the room.

Once we were all in position, Governor Kelly walked in, looked around, and said, "Well, looks like we have a big crew here today."

"I told you my family rolls deep," I replied with a smile.

I was blessed to have twenty-five of the most important people in my life stand alongside me as I was sworn in as secretary of administration for the state of Kansas.

My son, parents, brother, and grandmother—who, at ninety-one, had grown up during a time in which the color of her skin would have prevented her from accessing parts of the Statehouse, who was born just eight years after women had finally secured the right to vote, and who was now, in 2020, witnessing her Black granddaughter being sworn into a cabinet-level secretary position for the state of Kansas—were there. What I had written in my college essay all those years ago did not just hold true as it related to my opportunity to go to college; it held true at every pivotal moment of my life, and no truer than in this moment.

It was because I could stand on their shoulders that I was able to do the work that brought me to this point.

The Nineteenth Amendment, ratified on August 18, 1920, states: "The right of citizens of the United States to vote shall not be denied or abridged by the United States or by any State on account of sex."[6] However, Black women had to fight several more decades to ensure the right of Black women to vote in every state.

While we joked about the competition between the Chiefs parade and my ceremony, the gravitas of this moment was not lost on me or my family, and neither was the joy. My aunts, uncles, cousins, godparents, and closest friends showed up to share in that joy. I was so proud of Xavier, who was ten at the time, as he stood before me, steadily holding the Bible on which I pledged my commitment to the state of Kansas.

---

6 National Archives, "19th Amendment to the U.S. Constitution: Women's Right to Vote (1920)," National Archives and Records Administration, last reviewed February 8, 2022, https://www.archives.gov/milestone-documents/19th-amendment.

After I was officially sworn in as secretary of administration, we all went back to my offices. It was a proud moment to have my family see the Department of Administration sign, the portraits of Governor Kelly and me, and the flags of the United States and the state of Kansas flanking the state seal. It all felt so official; it gave me goosebumps.

Frank Burnam and his team had turned my office and the adjoining lobby into a mini banquet hall with long tables and folding chairs. All the food was laid out beautifully on the conference table. My assistant, Shelly, knew how much I loved chocolate-covered strawberries, and she had her best friend make trays and trays of them for the reception. I made sure there were chicken fingers on the menu, as that was the only food my child would eat at that time. My mom still had all her fancy serving dishes and centerpieces from her event planning days, so I had brought all of them in advance so we could set them up. There were lights and crystals. Over the next couple of hours, staff members stopped by to join in the celebration and to meet my family and friends. It was beautiful, memorable, and full of laughter and joy.

That day was one of many opportunities that my family and friends chose to gather to celebrate and lift one of us up—it's what we do. That day, they gathered to celebrate me and this momentous occasion. That is the kind of love and joy that stays with you and inspires you to soar higher.

As the celebration wound down and I had a rare moment of quiet alone in my office, I thought back to my first day, seven months earlier, when I arrived at the Statehouse for the first time as secretary of administration for the state of Kansas. Even my drive that first morning was memorable, cruising down I-70 so full of excitement as I belted out *This Girl Is on Fire* alongside Alicia Keys. I truly felt invincible and ready for anything, and when I pulled into the parking garage and slid my car into my very own parking spot, I felt so cool. I swear I was walking on air, grinning from ear to ear, as I crossed over the bridge from the garage to the entrance of the Charles Curtis State Office Building and then swiped my official ID badge that would open doors I never imagined I would one day open.

The clacking of my heels against the marble floor as I exited the elevator on the fifth floor suddenly hushed when I stepped onto the cushioned carpet of my office. Before me stood an imposing space filled with dark, highly polished furniture reflecting the morning sun streaming through the expansive glass windows that offered one of the most beautiful views of the Kansas State Capitol. I paused to breathe in the full potential this moment represented. But only for a moment—I just couldn't wait one more second to get to work. I rolled back the heavy wooden desk chair, its blue leather upholstery studded with perfectly aligned buttons, and sat. *Huh*, I thought, *something's not quite right.* I stood and attempted to adjust the height of the chair. Once I adjusted it to the lowest setting, I sat down again. My feet still dangled a good two inches from the floor.

This would become a running joke with my staff. Former Secretary Duane Goossen, who had returned to serve as acting secretary of administration until Governor Kelly filled the seat, stands at least six feet four inches tall—his feet reached the floor. But this wasn't just about physical height. This was also another moment in which I was reminded that my actual stature—just over five feet—and my perception of my stature were not in alignment. I often believe, feel, and move like I am six feet tall. And then I look at pictures of me with a group of people and continue to be genuinely astonished when I am always the shortest one.

On this day, February 17, 2020, the day of my swearing in ceremony, as I was surrounded by my family and closest friends, I'm sure I stood at least six feet tall, and I was eager to continue leading my team down our path of being seamless and visible.

Three weeks later, on March 16, 2020, the state shut down in response to COVID-19.

CHAPTER 24

MONEY, POWER & RESPECT

"Money, Power & Respect"

What's the key to life?
Money, power, and respect
What you need in life

—The LOX, featuring DMX and Lil' Kim

"I want to be clear: The protocol for the legislative offices is to put their trash cans outside their office doors in the evening, and the housekeeping staff will empty them and put them back. This protocol will not be changed."

Part of my job as secretary of administration for the state of Kansas was to oversee the facilities and housekeeping operations and lead the very people who keep the State Capitol running. Even when senior leaders, such as legislators, and their staff members had the option to work remotely and insulate themselves from the pandemic, the facilities and housekeeping staff continued to show up and fulfill their responsibilities so that the capitol continued to function.

Housekeeping staff members are hardworking professionals who are some of the lowest-paid state employees. They are professionals who try to clean and maintain the capitol without being noticed. They do such a good job that many legislators and their staffs do not notice or make any effort to notice these individuals or appreciate how they make everyone's job easier.

The legislative staff members were some of the first on the list to receive the COVID-19 vaccine. The Capitol's housekeeping and facilities staff members, who were in the buildings every day to ensure that state operations continued to run, were not on that same list. Their opportunity for vaccines would come two to three months later. For me, the safety of my staff members was imperative, and we adjusted our protocols as needed to decrease their exposure. Those protocols could involve something as simple as the placement of trash cans.

Many of those who worked in the Statehouse kept their trash cans under their desks. This required housekeeping staff to reach under those desks to empty the trash, often while staff members were still at their desks, when they cleaned during the business day. This created unnecessary risk and anxiety for my team. In a simple, intentional, and thoughtful request, staff members were asked to place their waste baskets outside their office doors when they left for the day. Housekeeping would empty them and place them back under their desks so that they would be there for them in the morning.

Individuals who worked in the Statehouse at various levels began to complain about having to do this simple task. Some only saw it as an inconvenience for themselves, missing the fact that housekeeping staff members were putting themselves at risk every day to keep the Capitol running. Their complaints demonstrated a lack of appreciation for hourly employees for whom being out sick for any length of time came at a very high cost. They are not afforded the luxury of high leave balances, and many work second jobs, helping to sustain their families. For hourly employees, being out sick can significantly impact their ability to pay their essential bills. COVID-19 exacerbated this risk.

When the housekeeping staff members heard these complaints, they believed they would have to once again retrieve the trash from under the office desks. When I heard these complaints, it was "Hell, no. My staff will not be put at risk." And that's when I found myself in the leadership's office unequivocally advocating for the housekeeping staff. It may sound simple, but it was truly imperative to give our staff members a voice, visibility, and protection. They heard that I had stood up for them, and that mattered even more.

This was just one example of "invisibility" that was not necessarily new but was escalated during the pandemic, and it was critical that I reinforced to my team members that they were deserving of the same respect as the legislators, their staffs, and every other employee of the state of Kansas and that their work was also important to the well-being of Kansans—which, as the pandemic rolled on, would become apparent to all.

Too often, the recognition and acknowledgment of individual, team, and department contributors are relegated to those with certain titles. As leaders, we have the power to change what recognition and acknowledgment look like—and I had pledged in the beginning that I would do just that. Our motto at the Department of Administration was Excellent Service, Every Time. To accomplish that, we had to be set up for success, and setting up for success came in many forms. The first, for me, was showing appreciation for my team—letting them know that I saw them and that others would see them too.

Prior to the pandemic, in September of 2019, I held an all-staff picnic for my department on the lawn of the Capitol. Every member of the team received polo shirts, lanyards for their IDs, and mouse pads, all branded with "Department of Administration," and we all wore the shirts and lanyards for a group photo on the steps of the Capitol with the governor. I wanted my team to know that I respected their professionalism and the work that they did. And for everyone outside of the Department of Administration, I wanted to be perfectly clear: We would be visible.

Now the long-term work of building the resources, equipment, and support my team needed to get the job done truly began. The Department of Administration oversees several functions for the state, including facilities and property management, printing and surplus, procurement and contracts, systems management, and the division of the state employee health plan. As such, the department serves as the lifeline and backbone to all agencies that fall under the governor's purview. And yet, between 2002 and 2017, during a time of cutbacks across all state agencies in Kansas, it was the Department of Administration that was one of the hardest hit, losing 35 percent of its workforce between 2002 and 2009 alone.[7]

When I entered my role as secretary of administration, the existing team members had grown accustomed to the lack of necessary support and resources to get their jobs done. It took time to build their trust that I would be true to my word and have their back at every turn.

The Department of Administration is responsible for all the guidance that governs how the state moves, what offices are open or closed, and what procedures are established; they are also responsible for

7 Kelsey Ryan, "Under Brownback, Kansas government kept shrinking. 'We've got a lot of damage to repair,'" *The Kansas City Star*, October 18, 2017, https://www.kansascity.com/news/politics-government/article179485646.html.

implementing those procedures. During COVID-19, the guidance also included masking, temperature taking, and other distancing protocols, along with the printing and dissemination of all COVID-19–related guidance and the signage needed to direct and inform everyone who came to the state buildings.

Under my leadership and direction, the Department of Administration and the Office of Information Technology Services met the additional challenges of COVID-19 and fulfilled my commitment to investing in critical areas. This included modernizing the state's IT infrastructure; advancing key projects, such as the Docking State Office Building and the Kansas Department of Health and Environment Laboratory; establishing the state of Kansas as an employer of choice through the implementation of new initiatives, including the launch of the statewide learning and talent management systems, the relaunch of the statewide internship program, the creation of the diversity, equity, and inclusion initiative, and the Kansas Women in State Employment (WISE) affinity group; and updating the equipment and processes of the state print shop, ushering in state-of-the-art technology and the subsequent honor of serving as a national model for printing.

As we continued to fortify our efforts against the pandemic, the very core of our democracy would be tested in extraordinary ways.

CHAPTER 25
GLORY

"Glory"

No one can win the war individually
It takes the wisdom of the elders and young people's energy
Welcome to the story we call victory

—Common and John Legend

n Wednesday, January 6, 2021, during Congress's certification of the 2020 presidential election results, a heavily armed crowd of supporters of then-sitting President Donald Trump forcefully breached the US Capitol.

Tensions remained high during the two weeks between the insurrection and the inauguration of President-Elect Joe Biden as the false rhetoric around a stolen election continued to gain traction. Law enforcement agencies across the country were warned by the FBI about possible armed protests at all fifty state capitols beginning on the

Saturday before and leading up to the January 20, 2021, inauguration. Three months prior to the insurrection, on October 8, 2020, the FBI apprehended thirteen individuals in connection with an alleged plot to abduct Governor Gretchen Whitmer and engage in violence to dismantle the state government in response to her COVID-19 restrictions in the state of Michigan. And five months prior to the abduction plot, George Floyd was publicly murdered by Minnesota police officers on May 25, 2020, sparking worldwide protests against police brutality and racism and the police's lack of accountability.

All these historic and intense events served as the backdrop to the time in which we were leading. Each event brought forth unique conditions that needed to be acknowledged, respected, and addressed—some more immediately than others. We were still knee-deep in COVID-19, and our day-to-day of governing continued to be consumed with doing all we could to keep people safe—mass testing; preparing for vaccine distribution; and opening and closing schools, public spaces, and government buildings as we thought best based on the most up-to-date information we had. People were frustrated with the always-changing protocols and sometimes-changing information, but everything about COVID-19 was unknown, and we all had to figure it out as it unfolded.

The week leading up to President Biden's inauguration, Kansas, along with every other state across the nation, had the added demand of preparing for a possible run on our State Capitol. Governor Kelly ordered the state office buildings located in the Capitol complex closed from Saturday, January 18, through Monday, January 20, 2021.

The Thursday prior to the inauguration, President-Elect Biden announced that he and Vice-President-Elect Kamala Harris would be hosting a national memorial on Sunday, January 19, 2021, to remember and honor the lives lost to COVID-19. The ceremony would include the lighting of the Lincoln Memorial Reflecting Pool in Washington, DC, and President-Elect Biden invited the states to join in solidarity with a lighting of their State Capitols.

Governor Kelly asked that we light the Kansas State Capitol for the ceremony. At that time, we did not have a system for such a lighting of the Capitol, but Frank and his A-team figured it out and made it happen as they always did. While I was still in my office that evening, Frank sent me a picture of our lit Capitol with the text, "We did it. The Capitol is lit." It was at once a somber and uplifting moment. I was so proud of my team and of the work we were all doing under Governor Kelly's leadership, and I was hopeful for our nation's healing.

> *We gather tonight, a nation in mourning, to pay tribute to lives we have lost—a grandmother or grandfather who is our whole world, a parent, partner, sibling, or friend who we still cannot accept is no longer here. And for many months, we have grieved by ourselves. Tonight, we grieve and begin healing together.*
>
> —Vice President-Elect Kamala Harris, January 19, 2021.[8]

When I finally left the office that night, I pulled up in front of the Capitol and took in the moment. Just as Frank had taken a picture and sent it to me, I, too, took a picture and sent it to Governor Kelly with the text, "The Capitol is lit as requested. And it is beautiful." Within moments, the governor responded, "I so appreciate you and your team and all that you all do that most people never see."

The following morning, Inauguration Day, January 20, 2021, all our buildings remained closed, with a few buildings completely shut down—meaning if you weren't a member of Frank's detail that day,

---

8 "Kamala Harris Honors Covid Victims In Nationwide Memorial," NBC News, last modified January 19, 2021, https://www.youtube.com/watch?v=mo3wtvmlQJ4.

you weren't getting in. I was at home, receiving regular updates from Frank and his team and from Highway Patrol (the office that oversees the Capitol Police) as they monitored all activity in and around the complex. There was a permitted protest scheduled for that day, to be held in front of the Capitol, which was being closely monitored. I would receive updates such as, "Looks like ten organizers, and they have identified a space they can go to." An hour later, "About fifty people have assembled, peacefully."

My purview also included the state's Office of Information Technology Services, and as such, I received regular updates from federal law enforcement around potential threats on the ground, as well as in relation to IT and national cybersecurity infrastructures. There were several of us at the senior leadership level monitoring and comparing information and assessing what, if any, steps we needed to act on.

I want to pause for a moment here so as not to allow the turmoil of the times to overshadow one of our nation's most beautiful and historic moments: the swearing in of the first woman, the first Black American, and the first South Asian American vice president of these United States of America.

As the inauguration ceremonies began, I pulled Xavier from his virtual studies in his room, and together, in our Kamala Harris T-shirts (sent to us from Jack and Jill of America, Inc.) and me in my pink blazer, pink and green Chucks, and pearls (because I am a sorority sister in Alpha Kappa Alpha Sorority, Inc.), we watched as Senator Kamala Harris was sworn in as Vice President Kamala Harris. Xavier and I had watched Senator Harris accept the nomination in August of 2020, during which Xavier had asked me why I was crying. It was important to me that my son understood, as much as a twelve-year-old could, the hope a Black female vice president of America represented—a vice president that looked like us, like me.

Thankfully, all remained quiet that day as it related to the inauguration.

Unfortunately, while those on the ground were working intensely to keep everyone safe, Frank and his team had to deal with state employees who were demanding to be let into their offices in the buildings that had been shut off to everyone. (Typically, even when our buildings are closed for a state holiday or federal holiday, if you are a state employee with a certain level of security, your key card gives you access to the building 24/7.) "There are state employees here demanding to get into the building. They insist that they have a right to enter the building and are refusing to leave," were the types of updates Frank would relay to me throughout the day.

I still cannot wrap my head around the fact that people who worked at the State Capitol, whom we were working so diligently to keep safe, were angry that they couldn't get into the buildings. We couldn't always disclose the details of why we made the choices that we made, and so we would find ourselves pleading with people to please trust us and follow the protocol we had set in place—a protocol meant to keep them safe in that moment. How could they not see and respect the gravity of the situation on January 20, 2021?

There are positions in which you do not have the luxury of choosing not to recognize the gravity of a situation. This was one such position. I, and so many others, were holding these positions at a time when our country was experiencing a perfect storm of relentless and unprecedented upheaval, creating a weight to this time of leadership like no other. As leaders, we were being pulled in so many directions, many of which were new terrain for all of us. As someone who is a policymaker whose purpose is to fix systems to improve lives, the heaviness of not being able to fix the divisiveness, the hatred, and the deaths that all erupted as a result of how the pandemic was perceived and managed just hurt so much. I didn't always know what to do with the heaviness of it all.

At the cabinet level, we all held so much information that we couldn't share. You couldn't go home and share it all with your family or call your best friend and tell them about all that was happening and how it was impacting you. And even if we could, none of them would have understood what it felt like to hold and to act on all that information.

I was in knots, I was frustrated, I was scared, and I tried my best to not let it impact my family life. But by the time we were a year into the pandemic, I knew I wasn't succeeding. "You're just always wound tight, DeAngela. We never know if you are going to come home and be nice or shut us out. You aren't fun to live with anymore." I knew my mom was right. More nights than not, I'd come home completely drained, and I would just shut down. The pandemic was everywhere we looked—on TV, on the radio, and, of course, online. It felt impossible to escape. I didn't want to talk about it because I knew too much, and I didn't want to scare my parents or my son. My dad was on the kidney transplant list at the time, and if he had any level of exposure, he would be removed from the transplant list until that exposure had passed. Any exposure could be the difference between him getting a kidney and not, between living and not.

Quick side note: One of the key people who carried me through this time was the governor's deputy chief of staff, Ryan Wright. When I say I knew too much, Ryan and I were right there together, many times with only the other person to discuss details with during those early days. We sat in the basement of the Disaster Recovery Center after our first briefing and just stared at each other, thinking ... *WTF!!!* When I left KU, I lost my Christina to my Meredith in Susan, but Ryan became my Christina at the state, or maybe I was his. This is important because he would walk alongside me in both the professional and personal struggles of this time. You must find your person in every setting and be that person for someone else as well.

Back home, I kept X home from school through the 2020–21 school year. He attended a small Catholic grade school, and when the school reopened in the fall of 2020, which was the start of his sixth-grade year, I did not send him back. I could not risk him going in and out of the house every day around other children and increasing my dad's risk of exposure or mine. I was already increasing the exposure to my dad by going back and forth to Topeka regularly during this time, but all of us who needed to work in person adhered to strict testing and precaution guidelines.

You must find your person in every setting and be that person for someone else as well.

My mom had to carry a heavy load during this time too, caring for my dad and my son. But we never really talked about the strain we were both feeling. My mom is a stoic "carry on" kind of person. If something needs to be done, she gets it done without fuss or complaint.

During all of this, I did my best to continue my workout routine, to get my hair done, to get a massage or pedicure every few months, and to do all those sometimes little but important things that helped me recharge. And I'm grateful for that community of support that accommodated my schedule and need to be as secluded as possible. I know that I wasn't always as responsive or attentive as I would have liked to have been, and I appreciate people's patience and understanding during that time.

I also did my best to lean on my personal circles of support. I know I can always count on the love and support of my family, and I consider myself additionally blessed to have so many girlfriends with whom I have deep and abiding relationships.

The women I call my KC Power Circle have become a deeply interconnected circle of support that has evolved over many years. This group of amazing women is a beautiful mix of my cousins, childhood friends, college sisters, and colleagues: Marshaun, Kisa, Christie, and Stacey, to whom you have already been introduced; Joi, whom I met through Marshaun; Julie, whom I met through Joi; Celeste, who, after we became friends, turned out to be my cousin; Latrice, who is my cousin but really serves as a big sister; Nikki, who is my cousin by marriage and friend by choice; Whitnee, who turned out to be not only Christie's cousin but also Joi's close friend; and Olayide ("O"), whom I bonded with as we suffered through our workouts at five in the morning together at the gym. O is the newest and by far the youngest member of our group, and this circle of women has welcomed her with so much love, just as I knew it would. No matter what is going on in my life or theirs, we are there for each other.

Pre–COVID-19, we'd have girlfriend night every couple of months. It might be a game night, a wine tasting, or a birthday celebration. In between, if there was a moment to celebrate one of us or offer support, we rallied around that person. Once COVID-19 hit, we, like everyone else, found ourselves isolated from each other. Not being able to share and socialize in person with these women created a void, and by April of 2020, I needed a way to fill that void. We began hosting Zoom happy hours in place of our in-person gatherings. That first month was the month of two birthdays (Stacey and Joi). So, I sent out some silly birthday party invitations—"Have your drink and something sweet to eat ready! We're celebrating!"—and mailed a gift to each of the birthday girls in advance so that they would have something to open in front of us all. And so began our monthly Zoom girlfriend nights.

These were not friends I could share the details of my work with, but that was OK. In fact, I think it was better for me that I couldn't.

This circle lifted me out of the stress of my job in a way that no one else could. All that was required of me was to simply enjoy my friends' company. I could just laugh and be silly if I wanted. Oh, it felt so good to laugh and just be me.

We had texted as a group over the years, but once COVID-19 hit, we made an official text group. Every day, one of us started the communication with a prayer, thoughts of the day, or words of encouragement, and from there, we continuously fed each other support, love, and laughs. There were many days in which I would text, "Today's going to be rough, y'all. Need your good thoughts and prayers!" and boom, my feed would be filled with thoughts and prayers that got me through the day. This circle of support was incredibly powerful for me during this time.

After the worst of COVID-19 was over, I was the keynote speaker at an event where Julie was the MC. In her address, she talked about the power of our circle and how it had carried her through. Until then, I hadn't realized that everybody else was being lifted and sometimes carried by the circle the same way I was. We are now even more intentional about celebrating each other. Not just birthdays and holidays but also new jobs, promotions, transitions, and family. All of it—the simple things, the big things, the mundane things, the silly things. It's Our Circle, and we now call it that. I think naming it has given each of us more power as we intentionally turn to Our Circle again and again, in good times and in bad.

The second circle of support of amazing women that I drew upon was a group of women who understood the challenges of my role during this unprecedented time. They knew what I knew, and they were experiencing the same challenges I was. Together, we were a force: my fellow madam secretaries.

CHAPTER 26

RUN THE WORLD (GIRLS)

“Run the World (Girls)”

Girls, we run this mutha (yeah)
Girls, we run this mutha (yeah)
Who run the world? Girls (girls)

—Beyoncé

“Oh, Amber might need our help,” Laura, Julie, and I agreed. It was January of 2021, and my fellow madam secretaries—Secretary of Children and Families Laura Howard and Secretary of Transportation Julie Lorenz—and I had been meeting together on a semi-regular basis since the fall of 2019.

But before I get too far ahead, let me tell you how what would organically evolve into a tremendous circle of support first began.

When I stepped into my role as secretary of administration, Julie and Laura were already members of the governor’s cabinet. Julie was the secretary of transportation, and Laura was head of two agencies, the Department for Children and Family Services and the Department for Aging and Disability Services. As the new person, I was reaching out to the cabinet members and arranging one-on-one introductory meetings in their offices to learn about their agencies, their roles in them, and how the Department of Administration could best assist them.

I remember it was Julie who suggested that we should get together outside of the office. "I think it's healthy for cabinet members to get to know each other," she said, before adding, "I do coffees with some of the secretaries. So, let's do that."

It so happened that our first meeting was at a local coffee shop called Juli's. That first coffee session together, we sat outside at one of the tables set out on the sidewalk and shared our origin stories. Julie had been part of the previous Democratic administration under Governor Kathleen Sebelius, so she had arrived in her current seat already connected to the political network of Kansas. When I shared my story of not knowing anyone in the current administration or in Kansas politics, her response was, "What? Nobody? How'd you get here?" By this time, I knew Reggie Robinson's role in bringing my name forward, and I was happy to have the opportunity to speak of him and my work in higher education and federal government.

After Julie and I met a few times, she encouraged me to reach out to Secretary Laura Howard. Laura's areas were complex and vast, from the administration of Supplemental Nutrition Assistance Program benefits and the state's foster care system to the state hospitals. She was responsible for two hefty agencies that spanned the state and all manner of issues. During our first get-to-know-you meeting, I would learn that Laura and I had a shared connection through KU's Public Management Center. Like Julie, and very unlike me, Laura had also been in and around state government and had worked with these state agencies under then-Governor Sebelius. How much of an outsider I was to the Kansas political landscape was glaringly apparent in the early days of meeting for coffee when Julie and/or Laura were interrupted by hellos and quick conversations by the many movers and shakers who passed our table, none of whom knew me yet.

As we continued meeting with each other individually, we'd find ourselves saying, "Oh, when I was having coffee with Julie (or Laura or DeAngela) the other day ..." Eventually, we decided that it would be best for the three of us to come together.

During that time, but before Julie, Laura, and I began meeting as a trio, I was also meeting regularly with Delia Garcia, our first Latina secretary of labor. Delia and I would grab breakfast in this little hole-in-the-wall diner right across from my office—they had the best pancakes. Delia was not a newcomer to Kansas politics either, having served as a state legislator with Governor Kelly, but like me, she had done a lot of policy work, primarily in DC. Delia (a "fiery Latina," as she would say) and I, as two women of color in Governor Kelly's cabinet, would strategize on how we could best show up in these spaces in a staunch Republican environment. For both of us, we were committed to moving through this space as our authentic selves, refusing to tone down or adjust our personalities. "They have to love us," Delia would say. "We're amazing!" Although I did not have the pleasure of working with Delia as long as I would have liked, I so enjoyed her camaraderie, and she was incredibly helpful to me in that short window of time, guiding me in which administrators or legislators I should approach and how. "Oh, they're approachable," she would say. "Go talk to them." Or if it was a more difficult connection or conversation, she would say, "If you need help with this person, just let me know."

Then, COVID-19 hit, and our Department of Labor ran into what many departments did—unimaginable issues around unemployment and the crashing of significant systems. During that time, as the leader of her agency, Delia would make the decision to step down.

Which brings me back to January 2021 and Amber Shultz coming on board as the new secretary of labor. I was the one who brought Amber's name forward to the governor's office, specifically to her chief of staff. Amber's name had been passed along to me as a result of my search for a senior IT leader. In addition to her IT background, Amber had also worked in executive local government management, so I was sourcing her for different roles.

When I understood that Amber was looking for a broader role than just IT, I passed her name to Will, the governor's chief of staff, thinking she might be good for the Office of Recovery leading our COVID-19 recovery work. To my surprise, a couple of weeks later, I received a call from Deputy Chief of Staff Ryan Wright, letting me know they might consider Amber for labor. I was still envisioning her in IT, so I was thinking chief information officer.

"No," said Ryan, "maybe secretary."

And I was like, "What?! That's amazing."

When the state made Amber the offer, I was asked to reach out. I had that phone conversation while, once again, I was driving down I-70 from Topeka. We talked about what it meant to be a cabinet secretary in this administration. But also—because I had been integrally involved in trying to stabilize the Department of Labor's unemployment system infrastructure—I made sure Amber understood what she was walking into. She was entering into a true crisis. We were still dealing with high levels of fraud in the unemployment system. I provided her with a realistic picture so that she would come in with her eyes open. Although she was clearly ready for the position, she still hasn't forgiven me for putting her name forward, but at least we can laugh about it now.

Our small trio—Laura, Julie, and I—had been an invaluable source of support for each other as we entered and came through that first year of the pandemic. Amber came on board on the eve of the pandemic's second year. Who accepts the role of secretary of labor in the middle of a pandemic?! "Yes," we agreed, "Amber needs to know she is not alone."

As we became a group of four madam secretaries in this time of extraordinary uncertainty, we decided we needed to commit to coming together once a month to support, advise, commiserate, and celebrate with each other. We began to meet for dinner on the first Monday of every month. We struggled to make our schedules work, and eventually, it was Amber who insisted we do. "I need this to survive. We have to make it work." And we did.

Seven months later, we would welcome Janet Stanek, newly appointed secretary of health and environment, into the fold. And where did the governor's office find Janet? In the Department of Administration, working as one of my directors. I brought Janet in to help run our state employee health plan shortly after I started in my role. I didn't know Janet, but her name came to me through a healthcare professionals list that was sourced out of the governor's office. Janet had worked in the healthcare industry as a senior executive in one of our local healthcare companies. When I was looking to change over the administration of one of my areas—the state employee health plan that we provide for all state employees, including those at universities and other public entities—I needed a seasoned and respected healthcare executive to oversee the department directly responsible for that work.

I would quickly learn that Janet was a no-nonsense, get-things-done type of leader—a perfect fit for the precarious state our state employee healthcare plan was in. Janet jumped right in and began righting the ship.

Just as with Amber, I would eventually receive a call from the governor's office, this time directly from Governor Kelly. This was unusual because information is generally communicated through her chief of staff, but because what the governor was about to tell me would have a significant impact on my work, she wanted to tell me directly.

"I'm going to be asking Janet to step into the role of secretary of health and environment," said Governor Kelly. She knew Janet had been instrumental with the state employee health plan, which was something the governor paid a lot of attention to because it impacted every single state employee. "That work has been exemplary," she said, "and I hate for you to lose her, but we think this is going to be the right thing."

Selfishly, I didn't want to let Janet go because she was amazing and her incredible expertise had allowed me to step back from the day-to-day operations of that department and focus on other areas. But more than that, I was so excited for her and so proud.

And then we were five.

This group of dynamic women began organically with a cup of coffee between two of us. And while we all had strong working relationships with our male secretary counterparts, and our forming of a group exclusively of women was not originally intentional, as we continued to meet and support each other, we recognized the value of our shared path as female leaders. I cannot tell you what it meant to walk into that restaurant the first Monday of every month and take a seat at the table with these women. Simply sitting down alongside them, I felt like a weight had been lifted from my shoulders. I knew that for the next two hours, I could share everything I was thinking and feeling, and it would be met with full understanding and without judgment.

We talked tactics, sometimes about something as basic as how to navigate our way through the labyrinth of gatekeepers to finally push something up the chain of command. We shared the challenges of being in the cabinet of a Democratic governor who was working alongside a legislative body with a Republican supermajority. No matter which party resides where, when the governor's office must contend with a supermajority of the opposing party in the legislature, it can be an incredibly tough and sometimes explosive row to hoe.

And we willingly served as each other's sounding boards when we were overwhelmed by the pandemic and the heightened social unrest that continued to permeate our nation. We lifted each other up through the particularly tough times and celebrated each other's wins, no matter how small. And, nestled in our booth in the back of the restaurant, we giggled a lot, letting our work armor fall away. We were a force, and despite the incredible challenges before us, we continued to move projects forward that had been stalled for years in state government, and we toasted every finish line that any of us crossed.

We also shared the added pressure of being a first-term administration. We all knew the gubernatorial election of 2022 was going to be a battle, and no cabinet secretary wants to be at the center of a news story that sinks a campaign. There were so many layers to the level of leadership at which we sat—a level that could feel incredibly isolated. To have this group of strong, brilliant, insightful, and wonderful women who understood like no one else could was a gift beyond measure.

Our voices, our circle, and our support were unmatched, unprecedented, and absolutely necessary. Yes, girls run the world, but it is an uphill battle that takes all of us to climb.

I would be remiss if I did not acknowledge the historical moment for women in Kansas government during Governor Kelly's first term. In Governor Kelly's own words from her January 16, 2020, State of the State address:

I realize, for those who have been around the Kansas Capitol a session or two, these annual messages might sometimes seem a bit routine. But tonight carries a special distinction.

For the first time in Kansas history, women sit at the helm of all three branches of Kansas government.

It is my privilege to serve as our state's third female governor, alongside the first female Senate President, Susan Wagle. And the second female Chief Justice of the Supreme Court, Marla Luckert.

Kansas reached this milestone at a fitting moment, as 2020 also marks the 100th anniversary of the passage of the 19th Amendment, which granted women the right to vote.

Anniversaries and new years are always important opportunities to reflect on time gone by, and on progress made. We have another such opportunity this evening, as we usher in not just a new legislative session, but a new decade.[9]

(Several months after my departure from the Statehouse, this incredible group of women came together once again to reflect on how we chose to lead during the unique time and space in which we served and the lessons we carry forward. I have included highlights of our conversation in a bonus chapter at the end of the book. I hope you enjoy this not-to-be-missed conversation.)

---

9 Laura Kelly, "Governor Kelly delivers the State of the State address," Kansas Governor's Office, January 16, 2020, https://www.governor.ks.gov/Home/Components/News/News/195/55?fsiteid=1&arch=1&npage=3.

CHAPTER 27
IF I COULD TURN BACK TIME

"If I Could Turn Back Time"

If I could turn back time
If I could find a way
I'd take back those words that have hurt you

—Cher

hy are we having this conversation? What are y'all doing?"

While my family had been feeling the impact of my stress since the end of 2020, I had managed to soften its impact on my staff pretty well in the first part of the pandemic. But by the time the end of 2021 rolled around, it was clear to me that the toll this role was taking on me was spilling over into my ability to lead effectively.

June of 2021 was the first time we brought all state employees back to work in their offices. And by August of that same year, we sent them back home again. And in October, everyone returned to the office once again. Sending state employees home to work remotely and then returning them to in-person work required an entirely new set of policies and procedures on how that would all work. All of this was in conjunction with overseeing the disbursement of the new COVID-19 dollars and the everyday running of the state. Each new day brought additional pressures, and the biggest stressor of all was that we had no idea when and if all the madness would end.

I remember near the end of 2021, when we were in a director's meeting discussing one of our projects. I can't remember the specifics of the project or if the issue was that it was delayed or just not working properly. What I do remember are my actions. There was no preamble on my part, no "OK, so tell me what we have." Right out of the gate, it was, "Why are we having this conversation? What are y'all doing?"

What I also distinctly remember about this meeting is the reaction of my team. They shrank back from me. Without meaning to, I had just questioned their commitment. I had questioned the commitment of the people who were working and pedaling just as hard as I was. I had questioned the commitment of the people serving in the trenches alongside me, doing their very best to keep this state open, running, and safe. They were not immune to the same stresses that I was experiencing. Seeing them shrink back from me stopped me in my tracks. Who was this person taking their frustrations out on their team? In that moment, I did not recognize myself. This was not the type of leader I ever imagined I would be.

I remember having individual conversations with my chief counsel and with my legislative lead a day or two later, in which I asked them how their people were doing. Both of their responses were very muted. "They're tired, but they're hanging in there." Their response made me think back to my interactions with them over the last few months, and I realized that I had been taking my frustrations out on each of them as well. I was stretched so thin that remaining present and engaged with my team the way I wanted and needed to felt like an uphill battle that I was clearly losing.

I felt deeply sorry for not leading with the appropriate level of care and concern for my team in those past few months. I wrote a note to each of them, apologizing for not being the leader I needed to be and for leaning on and pushing them more than I should have. I let them know that I did appreciate their hard work and commitment during such a trying time, and I asked them for their grace. I remember putting the notes in envelopes addressed to their home addresses and sealing them. I remember putting those notes in the mailbox one by one.

It was a pivotal moment for me.

In that moment, I needed to acknowledge that, while we continued to be effective in our work and we continued to accomplish so much, I was not showing up the way I needed to and the way I wanted to. My passion, especially under stressful circumstances, can turn into forcefulness. I recognize this, and I recognize that the bigger the title, the more care is required to not let that forcefulness turn me into a bully. I began to move with refined intentionality around identifying how and when the pressures were impacting me and recognizing when I needed to take some space to breathe and reground myself. Only then could I be equipped to pay appropriate attention to those around me and how they needed me to lead.

It would be in some of those moments, when I took some space to breathe, that I would begin to think about what might be next for me. It wasn't that I no longer wanted to serve as secretary of administration. I felt then, and still do today, that I was the right person for that role during that period of time. It was that I didn't want to continue in this role during all the pandemic-related, political, and social unrest that felt so far beyond our control and with no end in sight. I needed to feel hope that this unprecedented moment in time would come to an end, and it had become impossible for me to see that end while remaining in this role.

During those moments of stepping back, I would also make time to engage with a very small number of trusted colleagues from outside of the state—not to discuss what I was going through (honestly, even if I wanted to, I did not have the language or the strength to appropriately communicate what I was going through to anyone outside of my fellow madam secretaries) but to create time away from the madness and open space for me to envision the hope and opportunity on the other side of it.

These are those moments that we must learn from, and we must carry those lessons forward. I knew that, in everything that lay ahead, I would be intentional about controlling how deeply I let the stress and pressures of my job permeate the other aspects of my life. At least, I would try my very best to control it.

CHAPTER 28

I WON'T COMPLAIN

"I Won't Complain"

All of my good days
Outweigh my bad days
I won't complain

—Reverend Paul Jones

y phone buzzed, and I saw that my mom was calling. I excused myself from my Zoom meeting to answer. "Well," my mom said, "Dad got the call, and they said we should think about heading that way sometime this morning."

"Let's go," I said and quickly ended my meeting. Xavier and I were both home that day—me working remotely and X still engaged in virtual school. I packed up a few things for me and Xavier while my mom packed a bag for my dad and herself. We threw our stuff in the car and then drove through one of the worst snowstorms of 2022. It was February 17, 2022, two years to the day that I was sworn in as secretary of administration. The drive to the hospital, which normally took twenty-five minutes, took us almost ninety minutes. We were all coming to terms with the fact that this was really happening—my dad was getting a kidney. My dad had had two or three false starts over the past three years. He'd get a call that he was next on the donor list, but then nothing would materialize from there, so it was a long drive filled with all our hopes and anxieties.

As I strained to focus on the road through the swishing of the wipers desperately trying to keep up with the unrelenting snow, I just kept saying, "We'll get down there, we'll get a hotel room, and we'll just stay and figure it out." The hospital sat on a little hill, and it took me three tries to get up that slick incline. I had to take a running start just to make it to the circular drive, where I dropped my parents off. Fortunately, the hotel was directly across the street from the hospital.

COVID-19 protocols were still in place, so only my mom was allowed to stay at the hospital while my dad was in surgery and post-surgery recovery. Xavier and I checked into the hotel, and he immediately found a space to settle in with his iPad while I set up my computer to take meetings throughout the day and teach an online USC class that evening. Throughout the day, my mom would text with updates: "It looks like it's a match." (This was something the doctors could not be sure of until my dad was physically there and they could run tests to confirm.) "They're prepping him." "The surgery's going to take at least four hours." I kept a small group of family members—my dad's sisters and my brother—updated via text, asking them not to share too broadly. It wasn't until my mom confirmed, "He's back there, and they're putting in the kidney," that we could all breathe. Up until that moment, so many complications could have occurred to cancel the transplant. Now, after months of false starts, it was finally a reality.

When my mom called to let me know that everything had gone well and that she was coming over to the hotel, I walked across the street to meet her and caught a glimpse of her as she slid down the small hill from the parking lot. Every surface was wet and slick with snow, and it was challenging not to end up on the ground. Arm in arm, we pushed back against the pounding wind and made it safely back to the hotel. It was late—probably after eleven at night—well past visiting hours, but because it was a transplant, she had been able to stay with him until he was fully stabilized after recovery.

A potential infection was a cause for concern, so they kept my dad at the hospital for a few days longer than expected. My mom stayed at the hotel for another day or two before the streets cleared enough for her to easily commute the twenty minutes from our house.

Once my dad was settled back home, we knew there was a long haul ahead of us. The first year of a kidney transplant is incredibly difficult as the body tries to adapt to its new organ. Recovery required that my dad go back and forth to the hospital three or four times a week during those first couple of months for blood work as they worked to stabilize his medications. There were a few times when my dad's numbers were off, and he had to be hospitalized. My mom had to coordinate all of my dad's appointments and get him where he needed to be while also making sure she was back in time to pick X up from school. I could see the toll it was taking on them—a toll that was intensified because I was not available to help, since I was still working and traveling back and forth to Topeka.

My mom was also one of the primary caregivers for her own mother, my grandmother, who was then ninety-three. By March, it became too much for my mom to navigate both my father's and my grandmother's care needs, and she called upon her sister to come help. My aunt Von planned on staying for a month to help with my grandmother's appointments, but two weeks after she arrived, my grandmother became ill. After several weeks in the hospital, we moved my grandmother into the front room of our home, where she passed away on May 14, 2022. My grandmother was ninety-three, but somehow, it still felt so unexpected. My grandmother was a fighter, and she fought death right up to the end.

That's how 2022 started for my family. The weight of my work through the pandemic to this point had worn me down, but by the summer of 2022, I was a new kind of weary. My weariness was compounded by all the new challenges my family was wading through, along with the realization that my son was now a young man about to begin his eighth-grade year.

X had attended the same predominately white Catholic school since second grade. He had traveled through the past five years of grade school with the same group of about forty-five students. He was insulated within his little community, and eighth grade in a Catholic school is a big deal. There are significant milestones eighth graders move through, and like seniors in high school, they are the big shots on campus whom all the younger students revere.

I knew all those things were coming, and I knew I had missed a lot over those past three years. My work had been all-consuming, and it did not allow for the same level of flexibility with my schedule that higher education had provided me. I could no longer pop out in the middle of the day for one of X's events or pick him up from school. I was struggling to see how I could make it work the way I wanted and desperately needed it to.

I had a nervousness around X's transition from eighth grade to high school for various reasons. Much of it was because of common parental worries when children transition to high school. But it also had to be acknowledged that X was not just a young man but a young

Black man. During my son's first twelve years, I saw the reality again and again of the dangers specific to young Black men. I still saw X (and sometimes even today) as my little boy running around. But this child was already half a foot taller than I was, and I knew not everyone would simply see a twelve-year-old boy when he was walking down the street. Was he ready?

Doubts began to swirl in my mind. *Have I been present enough? Running back and forth to Topeka, working long hours, and then doing my best to shake off the stress of the day and be present with my family when I was home—was that enough? Have I given him enough time? Have I done enough to prepare him for these next steps? Have I introduced him to what he wants to know?* I had no desire to hasten his childhood, but I needed my son to be ready for his transition to high school the following year.

And that is when it hit me like a freight train that I was no longer showing up as the mother, daughter, or leader that I wanted to be.

The frustration and anxiety I had felt at the time of the insurrection and President Biden's inauguration in January of 2021 had not subsided. By the summer of 2022, it had mushroomed to the point of bubbling over. I was tired like I had never been tired before. I know the word *tired* is not enough to explain the depth of what I was feeling, but I am still at a loss for any word that truly describes that moment in time for me.

I knew it was once again time to make a change—a change that would require a leap of faith such as no other time in my life.

CHAPTER 29

I CAN SEE CLEARLY NOW

"I Can See Clearly Now"

Gone are the dark clouds that had me blind

It's gonna be a bright (bright)

Bright (bright) sunshiny day

—Jimmy Cliff

Just as I had to keep the news of my appointment as secretary of administration close to my chest when the position was first offered to me, my internal thoughts of leaving the administration would be held just as close. The gubernatorial election was just a few months away in November, and I would not leave before then. One, because I wanted to keep the promises we had made and finish what we had started, and two, I also wanted to show the strength of Governor Kelly's cabinet through the election cycle. I didn't want to leave any room for people to think I was leaving because I didn't believe in the work we were doing or because I didn't think Governor Kelly was going to win.

Once I had settled on leaving at the end of Governor Kelly's first term, I began my internal debate of what I would do next. If I didn't want anyone to know I would be leaving, I also couldn't openly seek out any new opportunities—that would send the same jumping ship signal that I was trying to avoid. It was an incredibly lonely experience. I remember sitting in my office having what felt like crazy internal debates on how this would all work. And then I began making a list of potential roles and opportunities I could pursue once the time was right.

Then, in September, one of my madam secretaries shared with me that she was considering a new opportunity outside of the administration—she wasn't ready to leave, but she was ready to explore other prospects. I wasn't alone! By this time, I had come to terms with the fact that I could no longer continue in this role and that it was no longer best for me or my family, but to be able to finally say those words out loud and to share all the concerns I had been internally debating for the past few months with another person who understood the facets was liberating, and it brought clarity to what my next step would be.

I had been working since I was fifteen years old, and through most of my adult life, that work consisted of a full-time job, along with part-time consulting or teaching, or sometimes all three. I recognized that in this moment, I did not have the capacity to show up as my best self, either professionally or personally, and that jumping to another significant responsibility would not solve the problem. I sometimes still can't believe what I decided to do next; it is so unlike anything I have ever done. I gave myself permission to take the break that I felt I needed to get myself healthy and whole again.

And then I began planning my *pause*. I went into action mode, determining how long I could financially afford to take a break, how long I would have access to medical insurance, and all the components that go along with an extended leave. It was like a pressure valve had been released, and I felt in control for the first time in a long time.

I did my homework, and I knew we—X, my parents, and I—would all be OK during my pause. About a month after I developed my plan, I realized that I hadn't shared it with my parents, and that realization stopped me. We all lived in the same house; my plan would impact them, so how had I not yet thought to share this news with them? This brought me back to my unilateral decision to leave DC for Stanford without fully considering the impact on Jason or Kelly. I would move forward differently this time, talking through my plans with my parents months before any change would occur.

When I did tell my parents, my mom's initial response was, "You're just going to quit, and you don't have another job?" And then she asked if I needed help, if we would be OK, and how this was all going to work. I understood her concerns. I had had those same concerns initially, and I had to remind myself that I had already worked it out and packed it away in my mind, but this was new information for my parents.

I reassured them that we would be fine and shared with them the consultancy and speaking engagements that I could take advantage of to fill any financial gaps. The idea of leaving one job without another to fall back on to give ourselves time to pause and catch our breath and to regroup is so foreign to most of us. We are trained to keep pushing through. And I wholly understand that it is from a place of privilege that I was able to even consider taking this pause. By this point in my life, I had the means to accrue savings, and I had access to alternative revenue streams if I needed to create cash flow. I fully understand that, for many people, even the thought of taking unpaid leave is not an option. I was grateful that this was an option available to me, and I prepared to take it.

After the election, once I was able to publicly share that I would leave at the end of the year (I had tendered my resignation to Governor Kelly prior to the election), it felt like a bit more weight had been lifted. But the strangest thing happened. Maybe it was just the political arena that I was departing from, but no one believed that I was pausing—that I was truly not looking for a new career opportunity. The common response would be, "Oh, you're going for something, aren't you? And you just don't want to share yet. I get it."

I would reply, "No, really. I'm not making a play here. I'm pressing pause for a bit."

"OK," they'd reply with skepticism.

Over my last couple of months at the state, colleagues, in a beautiful way, tried to help me find my next great role, sending me so many unsolicited suggestions and connections to other career opportunities that I was not seeking. On my end, I was navigating how to stay connected as a professional without a job. I no longer had a business card or a professional title. What would staying connected mean if that connection was no longer work related? In our society, intentional pauses are seen as a cause for concern rather than a healthy way to pour back into ourselves. I was determined to utilize my pause for the latter. But before I could begin pouring back into myself and my family, I had to roll up my sleeves as secretary of administration one last time and finish the work we had started.

CHAPTER 30
GOLDEN

"Golden"

I'm livin' my life like it's golden

—Jill Scott

I was late for my own farewell ceremony on January 5, 2023. My amazing assistant had done her absolute best to get me there on time, but just moments before the ceremony was to begin, as she waited for me at the entrance to the Capitol, my phone began blowing up with her panicked texts of "Where are you? Is everything OK?" She had worried that my last appointment of the day might cause me to be late, and she was right. It was a meeting with one of my staff members, who, while competent, did not trust their own competency, and that lack of confidence was impacting their ability to get the job done.

They were at a crossroads—even if they were not yet aware—as to whether they were right for their position or if it was time to move on. And as the clock ticked on my tenure with the state of Kansas, I attempted to counsel them through this.

"It is so important to me that you be your best self. And sometimes, our best self is in our current role, and sometimes, it's not. My job as your leader is to know the difference and to help you be your best self," I counseled.

I carefully explained that we had, at every turn, removed what they had identified as barriers, and we had created space for the work that needed to be done. Yet their confidence to get the work done had not improved.

"If you don't want to be here, if this isn't the right position for you, you need to make that decision as soon as possible. And if that is the decision you make, I will pick up the phone and will do everything I can to help you land where you want to be. But you're doing yourself and the department a disservice by continuing to lead without confidence."

While I have had these types of conversations many times over the years with many different people, it is never easy. And even now, more than twenty-five years later, these circumstances bring me back to my first real supervisory decision all those years ago in Guangzhou, China, and the responsibility I felt for my decision to let the young man who was stealing go.

I have evolved as a leader since my first post in China, but at the root of every one of these circumstances, I still want what is best for the organization *and* the individual, equally. I truly want everyone to have the opportunity to be their best self, and I will do my best to create the space, break down the barriers, and provide the support to make that happen. But if we arrive at a point where we recognize that the role and their best self aren't a match, and it is impacting the organization in a way that doesn't allow it to be its best either, a new path forward must be found.

Sometimes, it is simply not the right role or time for that individual, and as a leader, it is my responsibility to help them gain clarity—a sometimes painful process and one that often goes unchecked in government and in higher education. Instead of addressing the issue, people are allowed to continue performing poorly or are shuffled around between departments and divisions. This is not healthy for the organization, the employees who are working well, or the individual who is unable to perform at their best.

It was thirty minutes after I had begun counseling this individual that my phone began to blow up with my assistant's texts. I told my staff member that I really needed to get over to my farewell ceremony. They continued talking. I packed up my desk and put on my coat. They remained seated. As I came around my desk to leave, I invited them to walk across the street with me. They did, and as we entered the Statehouse, we went our separate ways.

I stood in the doorway of the ceremonial office, took a deep breath, and immersed myself in the festivities of what would be my last evening as madam secretary. The room itself reflected the gravity of the moment—regal columns framed the tall windows, and the Kansas state flag and American flag lined the walls. But what truly took my breath away was what my team had done without my knowledge. They had transformed this formal space into a visual celebration of our work together with poster-sized photos covering the walls—of candid action shots from our all-staff picnic on the capitol lawn with more than seven hundred Department of Administration employees, images from building renovation openings, and pictures of our team's minimarathon wellness walk through downtown during the pandemic. These weren't the formal ceremonial photos I was accustomed to but candid shots of real moments of connection and accomplishment that told the story of our four years together.

Joy was what I most felt as I walked into my farewell reception. Yes, I also felt relief, excitement, and sadness, but truly, joy was what I felt most of all. Joy at the opportunity to have done this hard but impactful work with an amazing team. The joy of knowing that what we had accomplished in the past four years would impact state employees and Kansans in positive and concrete ways for years to come and that Governor Kelly and her team would continue that work. There was also tremendous joy in having this opportunity to personally thank the many individuals who supported me and made our successes possible. And there was the joy of leaving with a sense of purpose and gratitude for my moment to lead in this space.

The room was filled with a wonderful mixture of people—staff from my own agency and others throughout state government, leaders from the smaller noncabinet agencies who had told me I was one of the first secretaries to really pay attention to them, a handful of legislators, and even people I didn't know well who had come simply to tell me they appreciated the work we had done. As I moved through the room, greeting each person with handshakes and hugs, my executive assistant, Shelly, who once again made trays of beautiful and delicious chocolate-covered strawberries, captured it all in photographs, which she sent to me the following day.

I'm not a crier—remember, I'm very good at packing away my feelings—but making my way through that room filled with all the amazing and wonderful people whom I had the privilege to walk alongside through such a time as this, talking with each of them, and viewing all the photos on display of some of the pivotal work we had done together was an emotional experience, and I may have shed a few tears.

The governor was so gracious in her remarks regarding the work I had done and the impact I had made. We both shared stories of how

I had come to the position and some of the trials we had weathered together. Standing there with the governor, delivering my last remarks in my official capacity, I was filled once again with joy. I had given this role my all and then some; I had left nothing on the table. I was proud of the ripples of impact that would continue beyond me, the leader.

CHAPTER 31

IT'S A NEW DAY

"It's a New Day"

'Cause the dreams that I've been dreaming
Have finally came true
It's a new day

—will.i.am

oooh! I thought, *this is going to be fun.* By the end of the third week of my pause, I had created a logo, a business card, and a website for the consulting business I had started in 2009. Through that business, I had served as a strategic consultant to a variety of organizations alongside my full-time work, but now, *now*, I had the time to build it up. It was fun letting my creative juices flow and putting my design and flavor on something that was 100 percent mine. I loved creating a logo that let my personality shine through, and the website provided the perfect platform to celebrate the impact of my consulting work—

something the high visibility of my full-time positions had not allowed. I ordered business cards, notebooks, and other fun stuff with my beautiful new logo on it.

I was on a roll.

Wait.

Wasn't I supposed to be pausing?

Maybe this is just what my pause would look like, I told myself—an opportunity to build my consulting business.

Or maybe, I eventually admitted, I was using my consulting as a front to justify my pause—using my consulting so that I wouldn't have to give up a title or be without a business card that I could hand to people, both of which would legitimize me during my pause. In a world where everyone asks, "Do you have a business card?" or "How do we connect?" it sometimes feels impossible to not equate that with your identity and value. There were times when I was asked, "Do you have a business card?" that I wanted to say, "No! I don't have a card because I'm on my pause." But I didn't because I was still struggling to define what exactly my pause should look like.

In the days ahead, I had many conversations with myself about how it was OK to not have my days all planned out or at least to keep a portion of my day a bit unplanned, but it was so hard to do. While I didn't have a job, I still had board responsibilities and had picked up a couple of small consulting projects. *This*, I told myself, *was necessary for financial stability.* Even though I had mapped out a financial plan and knew how long my window of time was, as a single mother whose parents also lived with me, I was nervous about not having a steady stream of income. My parents are 100 percent financially independent, but they live in my home, so if the mortgage isn't paid, if the lights aren't on, or if the gas gets turned off, it impacts them, and I had trouble shaking that fear of not providing. My schedule began to fill with these board and consulting commitments and the travel that went along with them, and still, it was incredibly difficult for me not to seek out more. More what, I wasn't exactly sure.

Then I went to breakfast with my friend Kim Alexis Newton, creator and founder of The Intentional Pause™ Project. That morning, as I sat in a booth in the back of the restaurant and waited for Kim, I laid my notebook out on the table. My notebook was overflowing with notes of the many things that I had either been working on or contemplating working on, and I couldn't wait to talk to Kim about them—such as my idea to write this book, to increase my teaching and speaking opportunities, and to serve on a few national boards.

Kim, in her usual amazing, relaxed, and thoughtful self, sat down across from me, smiled, and said, "So, DeAngela, have you really paused?" Followed by, "Are you doing the work you need to do to pause?"

"I think I am. I think I'm doing the work," I said.

"Girl," Kim laughed, "that means you probably are not pausing or doing the work, but I love your honesty in trying." She was right. I looked down at my notebook filled with my feverishly written notes about all I was hoping to jump into *now*, and none of it, not one word, suggested I had paused or had any intention of doing so. As I started to walk into 2023, Kim would be my pause champion, always challenging me to *really* do the work.

It is important to note what Kim was trying to teach me. As she would continue to share during my journey, The Intentional Pause Project is focused on helping ambitious women follow their dreams—disrupting them from thinking about what they should do versus what they could and want to do. She explained it to me in the simplest yet profound terms: "Ambitious women, in particular, need permission to pause. The research I did with ambitious women said that we need three things: (1) permission to pause because we see it as a sign of weakness; (2) tools to help navigate what we really want because when you're ambitious and smart and beautiful, you have a lot of options, but it may not be what you really want, i.e., the should versus could; and (3) strategies to fight fear because so many ambitious women don't go after their dreams because they're afraid." Understanding this was the beginning of the work.

Next involved defining what the work looked like for me. What was it that I needed to work through, to feel, and to get to so that I could be open to discovering what I wanted my next steps to be? That understanding sometimes showed itself in simple moments. It was a morning in late March (two full months into my pause), while I was sitting in my office with a wide open day between dropping X off at school in the morning and picking him up in the late afternoon, that I finally exhaled. All I had in front of me were the notes I had begun jotting down for this book, and I can distinctly remember feeling like I didn't need to add anything more to my day.

I had had many conversations with myself about being OK with open time, but I had never *felt* comfortable with it until this moment. The positions I've held were positions in which my calendar was not my own. While I had a say in who I met with or what events I went to, the when and sometimes the where were often dictated by external factors. To now have full control of my time was one thing, but to *not* feel compelled to fill every minute of it and to be OK with that feeling was, I discovered, a piece of the work that I needed to do. With Kim in my ear, I focused on the understanding that in pausing, sometimes, doing the work is *not* doing work at all so that you can get out of your head and connect with your heart. So, the work is actually removing yourself from what you should do so that you can connect with yourself enough to explore what you could do.

Unscheduled time in my calendar allowed me time to reflect and to dream—two things that are challenging to do when you are always running. Those unscheduled times also provided me with the flexibility to spend time with my family and friends in ways I had been missing for so long.

A big catalyst for my pause was my wanting to be there for X during his pivotal eighth-grade year. It was also important for me to alleviate some of the responsibilities my mom had carried for years. My mom had always arranged her and my dad's schedule around X's schedule—always making sure that they were back in time to pick up X from school, that X had dinner on those nights I was stuck late in Topeka, and so much more. Now, the number one priority on my calendar was dropping off and picking up X from school every day. I now also had the time to volunteer at his school.

Eighth graders are responsible for the annual school-wide carnival that raises dollars for a local charity. Xavier jumped all in, as he always does, and he built two different games for the carnival. Leading up to the carnival, we went to the local party store so that he could find just the right outfit for the day. Dressed up from head to toe like a carny game host with the mustache, the high top hat, the colorful striped pants, and the blingy vest, he walked around the house, practicing, "Come one, come all to the best game in town!" The morning of the carnival, X was dressed and ready to go early. Usually, for this type of event, I would be the mom who would drop off supplies or send money for supplies. But this time, I was there for all of it.

I was on popcorn duty, and from nine until noon, grade after grade came into the gym, grabbed their bags of popcorn, and ran to play the games the eighth graders had built. Every now and then, I could hear my son's voice: "Come one, come all ..." He was so animated and entertaining that his game had a long line of kids anxious to play. That was the beauty of the pause—being present for those moments in Xavier's life in ways I had not been able to be present before.

I loved these moments, and yet at times, I was still challenged to intentionally make space for them. But I kept doing the work, and some days, I was better at it than others.

The work during my pause also involved what Kim refers to as *walkabouts*—sitting down with people you admire. These walkabouts involved conversations with friends, colleagues, and friends of friends from different environments and sectors, including government, higher education, corporate, and nonprofit, that Kim and others introduced me to. These introductions were not for the purpose of landing me a job but for simply understanding and exploring new possibilities as I thought about my future self. These conversations would include thoughtful discussions about the work they were doing, the challenges they were facing, and the impact they believed was part of their day-to-day. As I listened, I began to gain clarity on what aligned with my spirit and my heart and what did not. *Again, not what I should do but what I could and wanted to do.*

As much as I loved higher education, I didn't want to go back into a higher education administrative role. Serving on Stanford's board of trustees and holding my faculty appointment at USC would provide avenues to remain engaged in higher education. The return to my role in government had reminded me how significantly the depth of scope, scale, and impact of that work can change lives. My career has always been tied to public service and in service to communities. Going forward, I knew I wanted to be in a space where I was able to influence and impact policy and resources in a way that would deepen the impact in our communities.

And then, the seat I was supposed to sit in next presented itself.

When I talk with young leaders, a common thread they share is trying to figure out how they get from their current seat to my seat. I always tell them, "You are going about this all wrong. Your trajectory is not linear." When we focus on the next and the next and the next, we limit our experiences, our potential, and our opportunities. I think this is particularly true for leaders of color because our natural progression doesn't always happen as it should. Instead of focusing on the next, we must intensely focus on doing the work in the seat we currently sit in. We must do it effectively, and we must connect it to our passion and the impact we want to see. When we do, broader opportunities will find us.

Instead of focusing on the next, we must intensely focus on doing the work in the seat we currently sit in. We must do it effectively, and we must connect it to our passion and the impact we want to see. When we do, broader opportunities will find us.

My transition from higher education to my role as secretary of administration couldn't have happened if my mindset had been limited to my next seat in higher education. By really committing to my work, my passion, and the impact I wanted to make in those moments, I had demonstrated that I was more than the seat that I was currently sitting in, and others had noticed and confidently carried my name into a new opportunity. Sigrid Emrich, my Foreign Service trade policy officer, had seen me and offered me the opportunity to serve as Charlene Barshefsky's deputy control officer. Reggie Robinson had seen me and carried my name into the governor's office.

With every role I take, I say, "This is the role I was meant for at this moment," and I go all in.

About five months into my pause, I received an email from my friend and mentor, Chancellor Doug Girod at KU, wanting to make sure I was aware that the Ewing Marion Kauffman Foundation was starting its search process for its new CEO. Doug said he could easily see me in this new position and new field that I had not previously served in. I, however, was not so sure.

I remember reaching out to two girlfriends who are part of my core support and whose thoughtful opinions I highly value. One was Louise, a childhood acquaintance turned lifelong friend, champion, and cheerleader. Louise was also from Kansas City, and she reminded me of all that we had come from and experienced growing up in Kansas City and all that I could do for *our* communities as I considered this role. "We all remember Mr. K growing up. To think, Dee, that you have the opportunity to continue his legacy… now that is something to seriously consider!" I think Louise was more excited than I was initially, and I love her for that.

The second conversation was with Marcela, whom I met in my sophomore year at Stanford and with whom I forged an immediate and lifelong connection. Over the years, she encouraged me to pursue admission when she was in admission. We had muddled through our doctorates side by side, and we now both serve as senior leaders in philanthropy. That late-night Zoom after we both put our children to bed, we pulled up articles and researched websites to learn more about the foundation and discussed what we found. Midway through our research, Marcela looked directly at me and said in her beautiful, melodious voice, "Dee, what are we doing? This is the role you've been preparing for. I am so excited for all you will do in it. How can I help you land at Kauffman?"

These separate conversations would serve as the catalyst for me to see myself as Doug had seen me and to reconsider this role as the one I was meant to be in.

The Ewing Marion Kauffman Foundation, based in Kansas City, has, for over fifty years, invested in organizations that increase opportunities for economic success, value collaboration and innovation, and catalyze systemic change. Its focus has been on education and entrepreneurship as the vehicles to do this work regionally and nationally. Philanthropy would be a new field for me, but I have worked alongside it throughout my career, including various programs at Kauffman. The idea that there was an opportunity with an organization with such a powerful legacy and community-driven mission, which served the same neighborhoods that my granny, my dad, my mom, and I were raised in—that is how one truly defines a full circle journey.

Sometimes, it takes being able to step away and to take a break to truly see what you need and where you need to be. My intentional pause provided me with a once-in-a-lifetime opportunity to bring all the collective experiences, knowledge, networks, passion, and learnings from my career to bear on the community that made and supported me. And so, in my role as president and CEO of the Kauffman Foundation, my next chapter began.

The process of finding the right person for the role I was accepting was a long, thoughtful, and closed process. Once the date of the announcement was set, my introduction was a quick but incredibly intimate and thoughtful process. The night before my public announcement, Susan Chambers, the interim president and CEO, hosted my soon-to-be direct reports at her home for a small reception. Over light glasses of wine in her living room, I met the leadership team in a setting that felt personal rather than formal. Each member introduced themselves, and I shared a bit of my background. Lo and behold, there were connections, such as Kauffman's general counsel and I had both attended the same local Catholic high school, O'Hara, a few years apart. He shared with me that there were many O'Hara alumni who had found their way to Kauffman over the years.

The morning of the announcement, we gathered all seventy associates—as Mr. K had always insisted on calling staff members because you work *with* him, not for him—for an eight-thirty meeting before the ten o'clock public release. The board chair, Esther George, introduced me to the room, but as we walked in together, I caught the eyes of several people I had worked with over the years in my various roles. There were knowing nods and smiles of recognition across the room—a reminder that Kansas City's community of changemakers is beautifully interconnected.

When it came time to speak, I didn't rely on a script. My notes, scrawled like hen scratch on half a sheet of paper, were just words and reminders of what I wanted to speak to. For me, in these moments, it's never about checking off talking points; it's about the feeling I want to convey and the connection I want to make with the people in the room, and that can't be scripted. I shared my story and journey, my deep roots in Kansas City, and what it meant to step into a role that was truly about giving back to the communities that had shaped me. By accepting this opportunity to serve in the zip codes and neighborhoods that this foundation was designed to lift and support, I was coming full circle to the very communities where my granny, my dad, my mom, my brother, and I had grown up. I had grown up knowing Mr. Kauffman's name, his face, and the work of his foundation, even though we had never met.

As I sit in the seat I am meant to be in right here, right now, I will once again be all in. But this chapter will be defined differently by the lessons of my past. I will be intentional about putting my well-being and the well-being of my family first. My life balance is not beautifully Zen and may never be, but I am more conscientious now about making sure that I take time and space for me, that I have enough energy and time at the end of the day for my family, and that I make the time to express my gratitude and to not take for granted those who make my life work so well. My son is masterful at gratitude, and I am happy to follow his lead.

Sometimes, I still move too fast. Sometimes, I'm still reactionary when I should be thoughtful. In those moments, I remind myself to be still. It is when I am still, when I am listening, when I am observing, when I am praying, when I'm thinking, and when I'm giving myself space to be in the present that ideas and insights are revealed, that opportunities are presented, that knowledge is gained, and that paths are forged toward a more equitable future.

My journey and my life's work continue, and I hope my story, my struggles, and my triumphs encourage you along your journey to dream a little brighter, push a little harder, and never define yourself by limits. Each of us is *made* for a unique purpose—to be fully who we are meant to be. Embrace it.

BONUS CHAPTER
I'M EVERY WOMAN

"I'm Every Woman"

I'm every woman, it's all in me
Anything you want done, baby, I'll do it naturally
I'm every woman, it's all in me

—Chaka Khan

Over dinner in my home six months after I had stepped down, the madam secretaries would share a meal, raise a glass, and discuss leading and learning. These are some of the questions my fellow madam secretaries and I asked ourselves and the responses we shared.

The power of your power: What does that mean to you?

I have seen leaders make decisions without thought for the consequences of those decisions on all the people impacted. When asked why they made such a decision, their response was, "Because I can." I don't ever want to be a leader who is not thoughtful, careful, and respectful with their power.

Power is about respect. I respect you. You respect me. Respect requires getting to know your people, who they are, and what they value.

At the end of the day, you can always flex the power of your position if you need to, but I believe that should be a last resort. Power is more powerful when you work to collaborate and gain consensus. Remember, whatever power you have can be taken from you in a second.

My power has been most valuable when I am what I call forever honest. *Tell people why you are asking them to do what you are asking them to do. Tell people why you do what you do. Tell people why they can trust you. Then back up your words.*

Power requires full self-awareness and an acknowledgment of what your nonnegotiables are, and then sticking to those nonnegotiables even when your back is against the wall.

Why have you chosen to lead at this level?

I love that at this place in my career, I can apply my forty years of knowledge and experience to positively impact Kansans across the state. This time in my career also affords me the ability to retire at any time. I think knowing that gives me more confidence to do the work that I know needs to be done.

Definitely the impact factor, but also the challenge of cracking the difficult problems. It's an opportunity to create collaborations that find solutions that translate into hope for so many people.

Bringing voices to the table. In my previous position, I continually heard from stakeholders in the human service field that they had been pushed out of the conversation, that their voices had been ignored for a very long time. This role, at this level, allowed me to bring those voices back to the table and to ensure every one of them was heard.

The opportunity to empower people to not only think outside the box but to destroy the box. In changing how we fundamentally think about things, we have the power to create access and opportunity for all.

What do you see as key leadership traits?

Agility. I've always put learned *at the top of that list, and I believe it is still key, but coming through the pandemic has made me recognize the importance of* agility, *which I would now put at the top. If leaders are going to discover entirely new ways of thinking about access, they must practice agility. And to remain agile, you must also be learned.*

Discretion. It's a leader's responsibility to use their best judgment to do what is right, even if it is not in strict adherence to the rules.

Courage. There are moments in leadership that require courageous action. Sometimes, you alone must take the stand, but it's important to also cultivate partners in courage.

What advice would you give your younger self about leadership?

Early in my leadership career, I put more emphasis on the rules than on the people they impacted. I would tell my younger self to approach her leadership roles with more empathy and to view situations more holistically, not just based on the rule book.

Find your champions—the people who lift you up, who build you up—and let them support you, sing your praises, and bring your name into the rooms you want to be in.

I would offer my younger self advice on navigating my confidence. Even as a kid, I was confident in who I was and what I brought to the table, which I see as a real strength. But I have learned over time, when leading, to be careful of too much confidence, which can give others the impression that I am the only person in the room who can do the job right. The team's confidence is just as important as my own for our success.

Be prepared to get knocked down and then get right back up. You will be stronger for it.

I'm a people pleaser and a hard worker. There are pros and cons to both of those attributes. People pleasing can foster collaboration, and it can also lead to over-compromising. Find the balance. Working hard can lead to great success, and it can also mean giving up important things. Find the balance.

Don't let your work and your accomplishments become your identity. They are what you do, not who you are.

Expose yourself to people who are different from you, people who have experiences that are different from yours.

Don't be afraid to take risks, even if it means you fall.

Set your own standards to live by and stick to them. If you do, everything will be OK.

ACKNOWLEDGMENTS

WIND BENEATH MY WINGS

"Wind Beneath My Wings"

I can fly higher than an eagle
For you are the wind beneath my wings

—Bette Midler

This is for Xavier—always and forever.

My parents, Jerome and Mary, I owe you everything. And my brother, Jason, I don't care what you say … *you* are truly the wind beneath *my* wings.

This book is also dedicated to the legacy and memory of Ambassador Ruth A. Davis, whose model of excellence has inspired me and countless others to always strive to be our very best selves in service to others. We will carry on, Big Mama.

To my KC Power Circle—Marshaun, Julie, Joi, Stacey, Celeste, Latrice, Nikki, Kisa, Whitnee, Christie, and Olayide—you ladies are true magic, love, light, and truth. There is nothing like this circle that has pulled me through these last few years. My love and appreciation know no bounds. Thank you beyond measure.

Antoinette and Alison, you are more like sisters than friends. Stanford brought us together in different eras, and our beloved sorority bonds us together, but the two of you hold my heart and my deepest thanks for allowing me to always be my most vulnerable self.

Marcela, my consummate sage and thought partner on so many levels, you have been with me through so many of these journeys. "Thanks" is not enough.

Gordon, thank you for your friendship, laughter, love, and frozen yogurt.

Dr. Laura (LTK), the highs and lows, twenty-plus years in. Thank you for listening. It has been my pleasure to be alongside your journey while you have been alongside mine. You're up next!

Louise, you are truly one of the originals in my crew. We have moved through many stages and phases of our lives together. I am excited for what is to come for both of us. Thank you for always being a champion and a guiding light.

To my editor, Beth Cooper, words cannot express my deepest gratitude for helping me take what was inside my head and turning it into a journey that I can share with so many. You stuck by me during my hard times, physically and mentally. I appreciate you for that and for making my story stronger. I'm ready for book two when you are!

To my early feedback crew—Deborah, Renee, and Stacey—your feedback and encouragement kept me going. You all mean the world to me. Thank you for the push and, most importantly, the love.

The Butter Sisters—Jan, Shirley, and Jeanette—thank you for always being true supporters on my journey, for always lifting me, and for always answering my phone calls.

James Jordan, you are one of the best—always there to support and listen to me. Thank you on so many levels.

Kevin and Jason, brothers I truly cherish, you two have a special place in my heart. I always appreciate how you show up, support me, and challenge me to think deeper, harder, and wiser.

Ryan, I could not have made it through so much without you. Your support and lift were genuine, and helping me pick out my new ride was icing on the cake. British racing green for the *win*!

Dr. Harper, my thanks are deep and wide for all you have been on my journey. You never doubted me, and you continue to open doors. You are appreciated.

Qiana, you helped in big and small ways just by being you and making important connections. Thank you.

Kim, without your Intentional Pause, I truly would not have had the capacity to start my book. Thank you for everything.

Governor Laura Kelly, thank you for the opportunity to lead alongside you. You are one of the most amazing leaders I have ever encountered.

To my fellow madam secretaries—Laura, Julie, Amber, and Janet—you are simply the *best*! It is an honor to have served with each of you and to continue to call you friends.

Leigh Ann, who makes the best cup of coffee with laughter and love, thank you for your unwavering friendship.

Susan (Ms. Susie), you are always there to provide feedback and be a thought partner, always with a smile or the best meme. Thank you.

Saidah, thank you for always being there for a call, a hike, or a great meal. You are one of a kind, and I truly appreciate all your support.

To all my godparents—Sharon and Tommy, Connie and Dave, and the Beenes—thank you for supporting me since the beginning.

Michelle, my cousin and continuous supporter, your support and your journey are an inspiration.

Jon, you are a friend later in life, and I cherish that the most. Thank you for just checking on me because, as we have established, *they not like us.*

Reggie and Danny, you two are amazing, and I thank you for being a great sounding board on so many issues.

Erika Kendrick, thank you for being a cheerleader for this book before I even began and for sharing every experience and resource you had.

Julie, you shared your craft with me early on, and I thank you, as I would not have known where to start without you.

To the families of Reggie Robinson, Dr. Richard Hope, and Ambassador Ruth A. Davis, thank you for sharing them with me. They are a part of me that I carry each and every day. Because of them, I am. Each will be missed beyond measure.

To the former Laya Center (Toyia and Joe) and BarNone Training (Wilson and Jackie, in particular) teams, thank you both for keeping my mind, body, and spirit balanced throughout this journey and for being my physical sanctuaries.

To my lovely ladies of Alpha Kappa Alpha Sorority, Inc., and the mothers of Jack and Jill of America, Inc., especially the Johnson County Chapter, thank you for the love, support, and encouragement through the years. You are the best.

Special thanks to my Stanford family near and far, with deep appreciation for the #ChocolateCardinal nation. There are too many to name, but each holds a special place in my journey.

My sincerest thank you and appreciation for those who paved the way on my foreign service journey. You taught us how to lead at the highest levels—Amb. Aurelia E. Brazeal, Amb. Harriet Elam-Thomas,

Amb. Sylvia Stanfield, the late Amb. Edward J. Perkins, Amb. Teddy B. Taylor, Amb. Susan Rice, and Amb. Harry K. Thomas, Jr.

Christopher Donald, it's been a long journey and I am proud to call you one of my best.

Shout out to my newest team at EMKF and the Board for their support as I finish what I started.

Thank you to my team at Advantage Books for believing in my vision and helping me turn it into a reality.

There are many more stories I could share and many more people to thank. I know I did not capture them all in these pages or this list, but know that I am thankful for so many in my life and journey. If I missed you, please charge it to my head, not my heart.

With love and appreciation,

DBW

ABOUT THE AUTHOR

r. DeAngela Burns-Wallace is a trailblazer whose life's work has been defined by her relentless pursuit of excellence and her unwavering commitment to breaking barriers. Throughout her illustrious career as a diplomat and higher education leader, she has shattered glass ceilings and paved the way for others to follow. As the first African American woman to hold pivotal roles in academia, public service, and now philanthropy as the president and CEO of the Ewing Marion Kauffman Foundation, she has carved out a path marked by resilience, innovation, and unyielding determination.

From her groundbreaking appointment as the first African American woman to cabinet-level roles as secretary of administration and chief information technology officer for the state of Kansas, Dr. Burns-Wallace has continuously defied expectations and blazed new trails. Her pioneering spirit has not only transformed institutions but has also inspired countless individuals to reach for their highest aspirations.

In this captivating memoir, Dr. Burns-Wallace shares the deeply personal stories behind her groundbreaking achievements, offering readers an intimate glimpse into the challenges she faced and the triumphs she celebrated along the way. Through her candid reflections and powerful insights, she imparts invaluable lessons on leadership, resilience, and the importance of pushing boundaries in pursuit of one's dreams.

With each page, Dr. Burns-Wallace's story serves as a testament to the extraordinary impact that one individual can have when they dare to be the first. Her journey is a testament to the transformative power of perseverance and the enduring legacy of those who refuse to be confined by the limitations of the past.

Dr. Burns-Wallace holds a dual bachelor's degree in international relations and African American studies from Stanford University, a master's in public affairs from Princeton University, and a doctorate in education from the University of Pennsylvania. She currently holds a faculty appointment at the University of Southern California.

The most important title to this Kansas City native is mom to her son, Xavier.

www.ingramcontent.com/pod-product-compliance
Lightning Source LLC
LaVergne TN
LVHW090559110826
845146LV00001B/184

9798891882997